Labour Law in Russia

Labour Law in Russia

Third Edition

Zhanna Anatolyevna Gorbacheva

This book was originally published as a monograph in the International Encyclopaedia of Laws/Labour Law and Industrial Relations.

Founding Editor: Roger Blanpain
General Editor: Frank Hendrickx
Volume Editor: Frank Hendrickx

Wolters Kluwer

Published by:
Kluwer Law International B.V.
PO Box 316
2400 AH Alphen aan den Rijn
The Netherlands
E-mail: international-sales@wolterskluwer.com
Website: lrus.wolterskluwer.com

Sold and distributed in North, Central and South America by:
Wolters Kluwer Legal & Regulatory U.S.
7201 McKinney Circle
Frederick, MD 21704
United States of America
Email: customer.service@wolterskluwer.com

Sold and distributed in all other countries by:
Air Business Subscriptions
Rockwood House
Haywards Heath
West Sussex
RH16 3DH
United Kingdom
Email: international-customerservice@wolterskluwer.com

Printed on acid-free paper

ISBN 978-94-035-0764-4

e-Book: ISBN 978-94-035-0765-1
web-PDF: ISBN 978-94-035-0770-5

Printed in the United Kingdom.

The Author

Zhanna Anatolyevna Gorbacheva studied Law at Lomonosov Moscow State University. In 1993 she received a Diploma in Law. The same year she continued with post-graduate studies in the Labour Law Department of Lomonosov Moscow State University. In 1998 she was awarded a PhD degree.

In 1995 she began working in the Labour Law Department of Law Faculty of Lomonosov Moscow State University on a regular basis. In 2001 she was awarded a grant by the Science Council of Lomonosov Moscow State University for successful young teachers and scholars.

In 1997 Gorbacheva studied European Law at the University of Nijmegen, the Netherlands. In 1999 she took part in a research session organized by the Central European University, Budapest, Hungary. She also participated in international seminars arranged by the Centre of Comparative Labour Law and Social Security, the University of Montesquieu, Bordeaux, France.

Zhanna Gorbacheva has been heavily involved in teaching both labour law and social security not only at Lomonosov Moscow State University, but also in other institutions (for instance, at the Academy of National Economy of the Russian Federation Government).

In 2001–2002 Dr. Gorbacheva took part in drafting legislation on industrial accidents and professional diseases. She also participated in making legal analyses on different drafts of the current Russian Labour Code. Under contract with the Ministry of Labour and Social Development of the Russian Federation, she made a comparative study on the legal regulation of temporary employment for the purposes of drafting the appropriate legislation in Russia.

Dr Gorbacheva has carried out scientific research with awarded grants, in particular, comparative research on the protection of social human rights in the sphere of employment under the Support Scheme of the Open Society Support Foundation (2001); research on social policy within the framework of the 'Governance in Russia Project' undertaken by the Institute of Law and Public Policy and the New York School of Law.

Dr Gorbacheva has been involved in research activities by the International Labour Organization (ILO). In 1999 she participated in the ILO project on contract labour. In 2000 she was responsible for preparing the ILO digest of publications on problems of the reformation of Russian labour legislation (which was composed of articles by prominent Russian specialists in this area).

The Author

Dr Gorbacheva participates in different conferences, including international and European congresses. Her work includes publications on labour law and social security (including contributions to the textbook and workbook on Russian labour law issued by the Labour Law Department of the Law Faculty of Moscow University and the Reader on Social Security). She is also a co-editor of several law journals.

Dr Gorbacheva is a member of the Russian Association of Labour Law and Social Security. She is an expert of the international centre on labour law at Law Faculty of Lomonosov Moscow State University, and she is involved in various research activities on Russian Law topics as well as European and International Law.

Table of Contents

List of Abbreviations

APR	Agrarian Party of Russia
CC	The RF Civil Code (Part I was enacted on 30 November 1994; Part II came into force on 26 January 1996; Part III was introduced on 26 November 2001; Part IV is from 18 December 2006, applied with additions and amendments, last of 2018)
CCEUR	Coordinating Council of Employers' Unions of Russia
CIS	The Commonwealth of Independent States
CPRF	Communist Party of Russia
FNPR	Russian Federation of Independent Trade Unions (*Federatsiya Nezavisimykh Profsoyuzov Rossii*)
FOMI	The Funds of Obligatory Medical Insurance, including the Federal Fund and funds of subjects of the RF
FSLE	The Federal Service on Labour and Employment
GDP	Gross Domestic Product
Goskomstat	The Ministry of Statistics of the RF
KTR	The Confederation of Russian Labour (*Konfederatsiya Truda Rossii*)
LC	The Labour Code of the RF (enacted by the RF Law No. 197-FZ of 30 December 2001, applied with amendments and additions, last of 2018)
LDC	The Commission on Individual Labour Disputes
LDPR	Liberal Democratic Party of Russia
LL	Labour Law
MEDT	The Ministry of Economic Development and Trade of the RF
MHC	The Ministry of Health Care of the RF
MLSP	The Ministry of Labour and Social Protection of the RF
RBUS	The Russia–Belarus Union State
RF	The Russian Federation

List of Abbreviations

RF CC	*See* CC
RF Constitution	The Constitution of the RF adopted on 12 December 1993, with followed amendments and addenda
RF Law	The Federal Law adopted by the Parliament of the RF
RF LC	*See* LC
RF PF	The Russian Federation Pension Fund
RF SIF	Social Insurance Fund of the RF
Rosstat	The Federal State Statistics Service
RSFSR	Russian Soviet Federated Socialist Republic
RSPP	Russian Union of Industrialists and Entrepreneurs
RTC	Russian Tripartite Commission on Regulation of Social and Labour Relations
USSR	The Union of Soviet Socialist Republics (Soviet Union)
VKT	All-Russian Confederation of Labour (*Vserossiyskaya Konfederatsiya Truda*)

General Introduction

Chapter 1. The General Background

§1. Geography, Location, Size and Boundaries

1. The Russian Federation (*Rossiyskaya Federatsiya*, local short form – *Rossiya* – hereinafter Russia, the RF) lies along the coast of Eastern Europe and Northern Asia, bordering the Arctic Ocean, between Europe and the North Pacific Ocean. It covers an area of 17,125,191 sqkm (6,614,800 square miles)[1]. The territory of Russia is divided into eleven time zones, from Chukotka to Kaliningrad Region. From north to south the country extends almost 4,000 km, and from east to west more than 9,000 km. Russia occupies one-eighth of the earth's land surface and more than three-quarters of the territory of the former Union of Soviet Socialist Republics (USSR). The territory of the RF incorporates the territories of its subjects, the internal and territorial seas and the air space over them (Article 67 of the RF Constitution).

2. The overall border of the RF is 60,932.8 km. Russia is surrounded by the following countries: Azerbaijan –with a border of 284 km, Belarus – 959 km, China (south-east) – 3,605 km, China – (south) 40 km, Estonia – 294 km, Finland – 1,340 km, Georgia – 723 km, Kazakhstan – 6,846 km, North Korea – 19 km, Latvia – 217 km, Lithuania – 227 km, Mongolia – 3,485 km, Norway – 196 km, Poland – 206 km and Ukraine – 1,576 km. In the east (by sea) it borders the USA and Japan.

3. Russia is washed by the Arctic Ocean – by the Barentsovo, Beloye (White), Laptev, East Siberian and Chukotskoye Seas in the north; by the Baltic Sea in the north-west; by the Black, Azov and Caspian Seas in the south-west; by the Bering Sea and the Seas of Okhotsk and Japan in the east. The longest rivers are Lena (4,400 km), Irtysh (4,248 km), Yenisei (3,487 km), Ob' (3,650 km), Volga (3,531 km) and Amur (2,824 km). The largest Russian lake is Baikal (31,500 sqkm). The highest mountain is Elbrus (5,642 m).

4. The capital of the RF is the city of Moscow with a population of 12,380,670 (according to a statistics on January 2018) *See www.statdata.ru.*

1. Free Encyclopedia: www.en.wikipedia.org/wiki/Russia.

§2. Political and Legal System

5. Until 1991 Russia had been a part of the USSR as the Russian Soviet Federated Socialist Republic (RSFSR). Since 1991 Russia has been an independent country. Currently the names RF and Russia are used interchangeably.

In accordance with Article 1 of the RF Constitution of 12 December 1993, Russia is a democratic federal rule-of-law state with a republican form of rule. Russia is also proclaimed as a social state (Article 7 of the Constitution), which is important for developing labour legislation.

6. State power in the RF is exercised on the basis of the separation of the legislative, executive and judicial branches (Article 10 of the Constitution).

I. The Federation

7. According to Article 65 of the Constitution, the RF is a federal state consisting of subjects of Federation. The subjects of the RF have their own constitutions (some have charters) and legislations (created in frameworks established by the Constitution and other federal laws). In particular, Russia consists of regions (singular – oblast), republics (singular – *respublika*), autonomous areas (singular – *avtonomnyy okrug*), territories (singular – *kray*), federal cities – Moscow and Saint Petersburg (singular – *gorod*) and one autonomous region (singular – *avtonomnaya oblast*). These are as follows:

- Amur Region (*oblast*), Arkhangelsk Region, Astrakhan Region, Belgorod Region, Bryansk Region, Vladimir Region, Volgograd Region, Vologda Region, Voronezh Region, Ivanovo Region, Irkutsk Region, Kaliningrad Region, Kaluga Region, Kemerovo Region, Kirov Region, Kostroma Region, Kurgan Region, Kursk Region, Leningrad Region, Lipetsk Region, Magadan Region, Moscow Region, Murmansk Region, Nizhny Novgorod Region, Novgorod Region, Novosibirsk Region, Omsk Region, Orenburg Region, Orlov Region, Penza Region, Pskov Region, Rostov Region, Ryazan Region, Samara Region, Saratov Region, Sakhalin Region, Sverdlovsk Region, Smolensk Region, Tambov Region, Tver Region, Tomsk Region, Tula Region, Tyumen Region, Ulyanovsk Region, Chelyabinsk Region, Yaroslavl Region;
- Republic of Adygeya (Adygeya), Republic of Altai, Republic of Bashkortostan, Republic of Buryatia, Republic of Dagestan, Ingush Republic, Kabardino-Balkar Republic, Republic of Kalmykia – Khalmg Tangch, Karachayevo-Cherkess Republic, Republic of Karelia, Republic of Komi, Republic of Mari El, Republic of Mordovia, Republic of Sakha (Yakutia), Republic of North Ossetia, Republic of Tatarstan (Tatarstan), Republic of Tyva and some others;
- Nenets Autonomous Area, Khanty-Mansiysk Autonomous Area, Chukotskiy Autonomous Area, Yamalo-Nenets Autonomous Area; Jewish Autonomous Region;

– Altai Territory, Zabaykalsky Krai, Kamchatka, Krasnodar Territory, Krasnoyarsk Territory, Perm Territory, Primorsky Territory, Stavropol Territory, Khabarovsk Territory; as well as some federal cities (e.g., Moscow).

8. The federal structure of the RF is based on its state integrity, as well as on its sharing of competences between state bodies of the RF and state bodies of the subjects of Federation. The Constitution explicitly defines the exclusive federal jurisdiction (Article 71). It also spells out the joint jurisdiction of the Federation and its subjects (Article 72). Outside of the exclusive jurisdiction of the RF and the joint jurisdiction of the Federation and its constituents, the latter exercises the entire spectrum of state power (Article 73). The Constitution includes labour legislation in the joint jurisdiction of the RF and its subjects (Article 72).

II. The Parliament: Federal Assembly

9. On federal level, legislative power is primarily vested with the Federal Assembly (*Federalnoye Sobranie*) – the Parliament of the RF. It consists of two chambers – the Council of Federation (*Sovet Federatsii*) and the State Duma (*Gosudarstvennaya Duma*). The Council of Federation consists of two representatives from each of the federal constituents. One representative is elected by the provincial legislative state body, and the other is nominated by the provincial governor and is confirmed by the legislative body. The other representatives (in total not more than 10% of all members of the Council of Federation) are appointed by the President. The members serve five-year terms.[2] The State Duma consists of 450 deputies who are elected for four-year terms. The last (seventh) State Duma was based on the results of the 2016 parliamentary elections, which were held using a mixed system: 225 deputies were elected on party lists and 225 in single member constituencies. Fourteen parties participated in the elections, and only four were able to overcome the required 5% electoral threshold. Currently the deputies of the main parties are represented in the State Duma as follows: the United Russia Party won the elections with 75.56% (340 seats), the Communist Party of the RF –9.4% (42 seats), the Liberal Democratic Party of Russia –9% (40 seats) and the Fair Russia –5.2% (23 seats) of all deputies.

10. The jurisdiction of the Council of Federation is defined by the Constitution. It includes approval of the Decree of the President of the RF on the introduction of a state of emergency, calling of elections of the President of the RF, impeachment of the President, etc.

The main competence of the State Duma of the RF is to create legislation. The scope of subjects which have the right of legislative initiative is defined by the Constitution (Article 104) (www.constitution.ru). In particular, the President of the RF, the Council of Federation, members of the Federation Council, deputies of the State

2. Constitution as amended by the Russian Federation (RF) Constitutional Law of 30 Dec. 2008 N6-FKZ, 'On Changing the Terms of Competence of the RF President and the State Duma of the RF'.

Duma, the Government of the RF and the legislative (representative) bodies of the subjects of the RF may initiate new legislation. The Superior Courts of the RF have the right of legislative initiative within their jurisdiction.

Bills approved by the State Duma shall be submitted to the Council of the Federation. If the latter rejects the bill, a conciliatory commission is created to overcome the contradictions. Then it must be sent to the President of the RF for signing and publication within five days. The President may also reject the bill. If the President rejects to sign a federal law within fourteen days, the State Duma and the Federation Council must again consider the law in accordance with the procedure established by the Constitution. Presidential veto can, however, be overturned by a two-thirds majority of the total membership of the Council of the Federation and the State Duma (Article 107 of the Constitution). In subjects of the RF, legislative power is vested in legislative (representative) bodies.

III. The President

11. The President of the RF (*Prezident*) is the head of the state and commander-in-chief of the armed forces. The President is elected by the population for a six-year term[3] on the basis of general, equal and direct vote by secret ballot. The President may only be re-elected to two consecutive terms. The recent election was held in March 2018. The current Russian President is Vladimir Putin.

The RF Constitution defines the competence of the President as a very strong one. In particular, the State Duma may be dissolved by the President in some cases; all members of the Government are appointed by the President, and the President may make a decision about the resignation of the Government. The President issues Decrees and other legal acts.

12. There is also a Presidential Administration (*Administratsiya Presidenta*) that provides staff and policy support to the President, drafts presidential Decrees and coordinates policy among Government agencies. The status of the administration is defined by the Decree of the President.[4]

13. The President also forms the Security Council of the RF and presides over it. The Security Council is a constitutional body. It is founded to help the President in formulating domestic, foreign and military policy. The Security Council is a component part of the President's administration.

---

3. The Constitution as amended by the RF Constitutional Law of 30 Dec. 2008 N6-FKZ, 'On Changing the Terms of Competence of the RF President and the State Duma of the RF'.
4. The Decree of the President of the RF 'On the Administration of the President of the RF' of 25 Mar. 2004 No. 400, with subsequent amendments.

IV. The Government

14. The executive branch of state power is represented by the Government (*Pravitelstvo*) of the RF. The Government of the RF consists of the Chairman (*Premier*), the Deputy Chairmen and federal ministers. The Chairman of the Government is appointed by the President of the RF with consent of the State Duma. Dmitry Medvedev is the Chairman of Russian Government (*Premier*). The Government issues legal acts on the basis of the Constitution of the RF and federal laws of the RF. The status of the Government of the RF is also defined by the RF Federal Constitutional Law N2-FKZ of 17 December 1997 'On the Government of the RF', applied with following amendments.

15. The executive branch of state power is also represented by federal ministries, services, agencies and committees. Currently the system of executive power is represented by the following groups of state bodies:

(1) federal ministries, federal services and federal agencies, which are headed by the President of the RF (such as the Ministry of the Interior, the Ministry of Foreign Affairs, the Ministry of Justice, the Federal Security Service and some others);
(2) federal ministries, which are ruled by the Government of the RF and which include their own state services managed by the appropriate ministry (e.g. the Ministry of Healthcare (hereinafter MHC)); the Ministry of Labour and Social Protection (MLSP); the Ministry of Culture and Mass Media; the Ministry of Education and Science; the Ministry of Natural Resources; the Ministry of Regional Development; the Ministry of Transport; the Ministry of Economic Development and Trade (hereinafter MEDT) and some others; and
(3) federal services and federal agencies, which are ruled by the Government of the RF (such as the Federal Antimonopoly Service; the Federal Service on Labour and Employment (FSLE); and the Federal State Statistical Service (hereinafter FSSS, or Rosstat)).

V. The Judicial System

16. The judicial branch of state power is headed by the following three Supreme Courts: the Federal Constitutional Court of the RF (*Konstitutsionniy Sud*); the Supreme Court of the RF (*Verkhovniy Sud*); and the Superior Court of Arbitration (*Arbitrazhniy Sud*). The judicial system of Russia consists of three types of courts, respectively: constitutional courts; courts of general jurisdiction; and courts of arbitration. All of these courts are represented at several levels, mostly depending on federal structure of the RF. General principles regarding judicial system are followed from the RF Federal Constitutional Law 'On the Judicial System of the RF' of 31 December 1996, applied with following amendments.

17. The judges for all courts are appointed for life by the Federation Council upon the recommendation of the President. The Federal Law of the RF 'On the Status of Judges in the RF'[5] states that judges may not occupy other positions (e.g., being a deputy), except those in the scientific, educational and creative spheres.

18. Constitutional courts may only be of two levels: the Federal Constitutional Court of the RF and constitutional courts of subjects of Federation. There is no obligation of subjects of RF to establish their constitutional courts. The latter may be created, and currently they exist in some subjects of the Federation.

19. The Federal Constitutional Court of the RF was founded in 1991. But the status of this court was changed after the adoption of the Constitution in 1993 and of the Federal Constitutional Law of the RF 'On the Federal Constitutional Court of the RF' on 21 July 1994 (hereinafter the Law on the Federal Constitutional Court).

The Federal Constitutional Court consists of nineteen judges. According to the Constitution, the judges for this federal court (as well as for all federal courts) are appointed for life by the Federation Council upon the recommendation of the President.

The Federal Constitutional Court has the competence to resolve cases regarding compliance of legislative acts and some agreements with the Constitution. This court is also empowered with the right to make constitutional reviews regarding the following legal acts:

(a) federal laws, normative acts of the President of the RF, the Council of Federation, the State Duma and the Government of the RF;
(b) republican constitutions, charters, as well as laws and other normative acts of subjects of the RF published on issues pertaining to the jurisdiction of bodies of state power of the RF and joint jurisdiction of bodies of state power of the RF and bodies of state power of its subjects;
(c) agreements between state bodies of the RF and the state bodies of the subjects of Federation, as well as agreements between bodies of state power of subjects of the RF;
(d) international agreements of the RF that have not entered into force.

It also resolves the following disputes over jurisdiction:

- between federal state bodies;
- between state bodies of the RF and state bodies of its subjects; and
- between supreme state bodies of subjects of the RF.

Complaints about violations of constitutional rights and freedoms of citizens can also be subject to constitutional review by the Federal Constitutional Court.

5. The RF Law No. 3132-I of 26 Jun. 1992, with following amendments.

The Federal Constitutional Court also has the right to interpret the RF Constitution on request by the RF President, the Council of Federation, the State Duma of the RF, the Government and state bodies of legislative power of subjects of the RF.

Saint Petersburg is the city of location of the Federal Constitutional Court.

20. The Supreme Court of the RF is the highest judicial body on matters which are resolved by courts of general jurisdiction (which include matters of Labour Law (LL)). It also offers explanations on judicial practice that are important to LL practice. The judges of the Supreme Court of the RF are appointed by the Counsel of Federation with participation of the President of the RF.

21. The system of courts of general jurisdiction in the RF is defined by Federal Constitutional Law 'On Courts of General Jurisdiction' of 7 February 2011, with following amendments of 2014. Besides the Supreme Court of the RF, it includes the Supreme Courts of republics, territorial, municipal federal courts and regional courts, as well as specialized courts. These courts are staffed by professional judges, with juries working in cases stipulated by law.

The majority of matters are heard by the courts of general jurisdiction of the lowest level (the courts of the first instance). Moreover, the system of Justice of the Peace was also established in Russia. The Justices of the Peace are enabled to resolve some cases which are usually solved by regional courts, with some exceptions. It has to be stressed that the competence of Justices of the Peace is regulated by laws of the subjects of the RF.

22. The Superior Arbitration Court of the RF is the highest judicial body resolving economic disputes. It also provides explanations on questions of judicial practice within its competence.

The courts of arbitration have their own special hierarchy. The specific features of Russian arbitration courts are regulated by the Federal Constitutional Law 'On Arbitration Courts' of 1995, with following amendments (most recently in 2016). The whole territory of the RF is divided into several so-called arbitration areas (singular *okrug*).

23. It should be stressed that in Russia there are no special courts dealing with labour disputes. All disputes connected with employment relationships, as well as some disputes arising from collective labour relationships, are heard by courts of general jurisdiction. First, the cases may be resolved by regional courts (except cases of recognizing of strikes to be illegal, which should be heard by courts of subjects of the Federation, including the courts of Moscow and Saint Petersburg). Justices of the Peace are also granted the competence to resolve LL disputes, with some exceptions (e.g., cases regarding termination of employment are heard only by regional courts).

VI. Local Self-government

24. Local self-government is established in cities, other areas and territories taking into account historical and other local traditions. It is exercised by citizens through referendums, elections and forms of expression of their will, through elected and other bodies of local self-government. The structure of bodies of local self-government is determined by the population independently. It is regulated by Federal Law No. 131-FZ 'On the Main Principles of Organization of Local Self-government' of 6 October 2003, with following amendments (most recent of 2018).

VII. International Relations

25. Russia is a member of many international organizations, such as the European Council, the United Nations, International Labour Organization (ILO), the Asia-Pacific Economic Cooperation, the World Trade Organization, Eurasian Economic Union (since 2015) and some others. The RF is a part of the Commonwealth of Independent States (CIS) and the Russia–Belarus Union State (RBUS).

VIII. Political Parties

26. The Constitution provides for political diversity and the operation of many political parties in the country. The Federal Law 'On Political Parties' was adopted in July 2001. This law guarantees rights to Russian citizens in the sphere of creating and joining political parties, as well as freedom to leave them. A political party must have regional branches in more than half of the subjects of the RF, but not more than one branch in each of them.

27. Today the following political parties have significant importance in Russia:

(1) United Russia: on 1 December 2001, an All-Russian party Unity and Fatherland was created during a unification convention of Unity (*Edinstvo*) and Fatherland-All Russia (*Otechestvo-Vsya Rossiya*) political movements. The new party positions itself as pro-presidential. Currently this party represents the great majority in the State Duma – Russian Parliament.

(2) The Liberal Democratic Party of Russia (LDPR) was created in 1989 as a Liberal Democratic Party of the USSR. In April 1992 it was renamed the LDPR. This party positions itself as a centrist pro-reform democratic party. LDPR proclaims a democratic state with a strong presidential rule and regulated market economy as its political goal. The LDPR economic programme suggests strengthening of the state sector, limited privatization and measures against unemployment.

(3) The Communist Party of Russia (CPRF) was created in June 1990 as part of the Communist Party of the USSR. At the moment of its creation in the summer of 1990 the CPRF had ten million members. Currently the party has around 160,000 members. There are over 20,000 local CPRF branches in Russia.
(4) The Fair Russia – Motherland Party (also translated as Russia of Justice or Just Russia) was formed in October 2006. Fair Russia is politically more to the left than the United Russia.
(5) The Agrarian Party of Russia (APR) was founded in February 1993. This is a left-wing movement that expresses the interests of agro-industrial workers as well as villagers and inhabitants of small towns. The APR was formed mainly on the basis of the Agrarian Union of Workers and the Trade Union of Workers of the Agro-industrial Complex. Agrarian Party is currently united with *People's Front for Russia* and *Russian Ecological Party*.
(6) The Other Russia pulls together opponents of the Government founded in 2006, and the widely diverse coalition includes notable opposition figures. It aims to restore civil control of power in Russia, to guarantee Russian Constitution.

§3. Population

28. Over the past decades, the total number of inhabitants has been declining. But past several years have changed this tendency dramatically, as shown in the Table 1.

Table 1 The population of the RF (million)

Year	Population
1994	148.2
1997	147.1
2002	145.2
2005	143.5
2006	142.8
2007	142.0
2009	141.9
2011	142.9
2012	143.0
2013	143.0
2015	146.5
2017	146.9

Source: RF Rosstat www.gks.ru.

29. The number of female inhabitants is higher. For example, in 2017 female inhabitants were 78.7 million (54% of the population), whereas male inhabitants were 68.2 million (46% of the population). The same proportion can be seen in 2018.

30. Russia is a multinational state. People of more than 100 nationalities and ethnic groups live in its territory. The majority of the population is Russian and it constitutes more than four-fifths of the entire population (81.5%). There are also Tatar (3.8%), Ukrainian (3%), Chuvash (1.2%), Bashkir (0.9%), Belarusian (0.8%), Moldavian (0.7%) and some other ethnic groups (8.1%) in the RF.

31. The state language of the RF throughout its territory is Russian (Article 68 of the Constitution). The republics have the right to institute their own state languages which are used alongside the state language of the RF in bodies of state power, bodies of local self-government and state institutions of the republics. The Constitution also guarantees all the population the right to preserve their native language and to create the conditions for its study and development.

Russian language belongs to the Eastern group of Slavonic languages of the Indo-European family of languages. The written language is based on the Russian alphabet.

The Federal Law No. 53-FZ 'On State Language of the RF' was signed by the President on 1 June 2005.

Russian is the working language of the executive bodies of the CIS and the RBUS. Russian is one of the six official languages of the United Nations.

32. Historically, the RF is a multi-confessional state formation. It should be noted that during some periods of the USSR, religious life was suppressed. From the beginning of the 1990s, religious life in the country acquired more freedom. As a consequence, the Constitution guaranteed legal equality of all religious associations irrespective of their confessional affiliation. Later the Federal Law No. 1125-FZ of 26 September 1997 'On Freedom of Conscience and Religious Associations' was adopted. Currently it is applied with following amendments.

Significant changes have occurred in the religious-confessional structure of Russia during the past fifteen to twenty years. Along with the faiths that are traditional in Russia – Orthodoxy, Islam, Buddhism, Judaism and Catholicism – there are also numerous religious currents and sects (such as Lutherans, Protestants, Old Believers, followers of Zoroastrianism, fire-worshippers, Baptists, Adventists, Pentecostalists and so on). As per the number of believers, the largest religious groups in Russia are: Christianity (first of all Orthodoxy as traditional religion for Russia), Islam, Buddhism, Judaism and Catholicism.

§4. The Economy

33. The main features of contemporary Russia should be explained in connection with processes of transition (transformation) of economy. In the mid and late

1980s, General Secretary M. Gorbachev introduced glasnost (open society) and perestroika (restructuring) as an attempt to modernize the Communist system of rule. Since then, Russia has developed in its efforts to build a market economy, to replace the strict social, political and economic controls of the Communist period and, as consequence, to change the methods and content of state regulation.

The above processes changed the nature of all relations within the society, including in the social sphere.

I. Starting Reforms

34. One of the most distinguishing features of the Soviet (of past USSR) economy was an extremely high concentration of production at major enterprises, a system of command distribution of cheap materials and fuel and energy resources, total price regulation and an almost complete isolation from the international economic market. In the late 1980s, the system of command distribution started to weaken as a result of Mikhail Gorbachev's reforms. Economic ties between enterprises and economic sectors broke up. That disorganized the economic life in the country causing shortages of many commodities, including basic necessities. Economists used to characterize the late 1980s/early 1990s as a period of crisis of the centralized model of management before the start of market reforms.

35. After the disintegration of the USSR, the first Russian President Boris Yeltsin and the Government led by Prime Minister Yegor Gaidar started liberal reforms. The state abandoned its control over wholesale and retail prices for 90% of commodities under a Decree on 'price liberalization' issued on 2 January 1992. The state monopoly on foreign trade was also abolished the same year. The rouble became convertible. As a result, Russia exceeded the Soviet parameters in the exports of oil, gas, ferrous metals, timber and other raw materials. That increased the share of raw materials in Russian exports compared even to the Soviet era and consolidated Russia's status of exporter of raw materials.

II. Privatization

36. Privatization was the next step of economic reform in the RF. It was carried out in phases from late 1991 to late 1994. At first, so-called vouchers with a nominal value of RUB 10,000 were distributed among the population. Their value was determined by dividing the book value of all Russian property by the total number of Russian citizens. The process of turning enterprises into joint-stock companies started at the same time. About 2,000 cheque investment foundations were set up to swap vouchers for shares. However, the stocks of very few and not very attractive state enterprises were put for sale during the early auctions. As a result, millions of people became holders of shares which do not have any value even today.

The first period of privatization was over in July 1994. Many enterprises were on the edge of bankruptcy. As a consequence, they were sold at inappropriate prices.

Part of the shares was handed over to work collectives, while the rest were sold at auctions. Foreign companies were not given access to auctions until late 1994.

The Russian economy started stabilizing in 1995. The economic decline slowed down noticeably and some growth was noted in industries such as metallurgy, power engineering and chemistry. Inflation began to decline.

III. Crisis in 1998

37. In 1998 Russian economy was shattered by the worst economic crisis in Russia's recent history. The rouble plunged three times against the dollar in the course of several days. One of the reasons for the crisis was a sharp fall in oil prices – one of the major sources of Russian budget revenue. The Gross Domestic Product (GDP) in 1998 decreased by 4.9% as compared to 1997. Inflation stood at 84.4% in 1998. The official dollar exchange rate grew from RUB 5.96 to RUB 20.62 per dollar. The crisis also led to degradation of the commercial bank system.

Nevertheless, the country's foreign trade increased considerably to reach a surplus of 32.5 billion dollars in 1999. As prices rose for foreign imports, Russian goods became more competitive. In 1999 GDP grew at a rate of 3% largely due to export-oriented or import-substitution industries. Industrial output grew by 7.5%. The effects of dollar devaluation lasted all through 2000, characterized by the best economic indicators since the late 1960s. The GDP grew by 7.5%, industrial output by 12%, exports by 40%, foreign investments in economy by 18% and the Central Bank gold and currency reserves reached 30 billion dollars.

38. The current Russian economy is based on the principle of equality of different types of property. It was set in place by the RSFSR Law 'On Property in the RSFSR' of 24 December 1990 which reinstated the institution of private property. The subsequent RSFSR Law 'On Enterprises and Entrepreneurial Activities' of 25 December 1990 established a legal framework for the emergence and further development of various types of legal persons unknown to the legislation previously in force. Now these aspects are regulated by the Civil Code of the RF (CC).

Despite numerous attempts to develop small and medium businesses, their share in production output is small and amounts to a few per cent.

IV. Gross Domestic Product

39. For the past years economic growth has been indicated. The year 2002 was the fourth consecutive year of growth for Russian economy. As compared to 2002, in 2003 the GDP increased by 7.3%. In 2004 the GDP grew steadily and achieved in the end of 2004 as a whole RUB 12 trillion 164.4 billion (around USD 1.282 trillion), which was 7% more than the year 2003.[6]

The followed year were recognized as the years of economic growth too. In 2007 the GDP was accounted as RUB 23065.9 milliard (USD 1.4 trillion), which was

6. Data provided by the Ministry of Economic Development and Trade. *See* www.economy.gov.ru.

107.8% of the GDP in 2006. During past years, the GDP continued to grew steadily and was accounted in 2011 as RUB 54,586 billion, whereas in 2017 already RUB 92,037 billion (around USD 1.53 trillion)[7].

40. In 2016 GDP composition by sector was as follows: agriculture – 5.4%, industry – 38% and services – 57.1%. The economic growth was primarily driven by services and sales of goods.

41. Among regions significant (by more than 20%) production growth was registered in the Moscow, Kaliningrad, Leningrad (*Leningradskaya Oblast*), Rostov and Kamchatka Regions.

V. Main Industries

42. The main Russian industries are the following: the complete range of mining and extractive industries producing coal, oil, gas, chemicals and metals; all forms of machine building from rolling mills to high-performance aircraft and space vehicles; shipbuilding; road and rail transportation equipment; communications equipment; agricultural machinery, tractors, and construction equipment; electric power generating and transmitting equipment; medical and scientific instruments; and consumer durables, textiles, foodstuffs and handicrafts.

VI. Exports and Imports

43. Oil, natural gas, metals and timber still account around 80% of exports. The commodity structure of Russian exports in 2016 was still largely raw materials oriented. For example, mineral products accounted for 62.9% of all export metals and precious stones for 13.5%, as well as chemical products for around 8.5%. At the same time machinery, equipment and transport means were estimated as 7.3% of all exports in 2016. In total exports volume of Russia in 2016, the largest share accounted for the following countries: the Netherlands – 10.2%; China – 9.8%; Germany – 7.4%; Belarus – 4.9%;Italy – 4.2%; USA – 3.3%; Ukraine – 2.2%; and France – 1.7%.

In 2016 to imports belonged vehicles, machinery and transport means, as well as equipment (47.4%), chemical products (18.5%); meat, fruit and other foodstuffs and agricultural raw materials (13.7%) and some other goods. Russia's main import partners are China (20.9%), Germany (10.7%), Belarus (5.2%), Japan (3.7%), France (4.7%), Ukraine (2.2%), the USA (6.0%) and Italy (4.3%).

7. *Source: RF Rosstat available at* www.gks.ru.

VII. Income per Capita

44. The volume of the most important social guarantees provided by the state – minimum wages, benefits and stipends still falls far below the minimum subsistence concerning some cases. The minimum wage as stated by legislation no longer performs its economic, protective and social functions. At the same time, the significant feature of the Russian economy still remains as so-called black (not official) payments for employees that are often calculated as bigger parts of salaries.

45. Generally, during 1998–2003 the GDP of Russia has grown 26%, while real income per capita grew by only 8%. The State Statistics Committee (currently – Rosstat) announced that approximately 12.5% of Russians remained below the federally designated subsistence level in 2007.

Last statistical data shows that the amount of population with the income per capita below the officially established survival minimum was rising during the past years and has reached 13.3 percent in 2016 (as compared to 10.8% in 2013). Data by the MEDT. *See* www.economy.gov.ru; www.focus-economics.com.

VIII. Inflation

46. One of the features of the Russian economy is inflation. On an average the inflation rate in Russia was 125.36% during the period of time from 1991 to 2018, reaching the highest level in December 1991. The inflation rate accelerated at the beginning of the year 2008, reaching 2.3% in January (*v.* 1.7% in the same period of 2007). The growth in consumer prices in January 2008 was around 1.3% as compared to December 2007 (1.9% concerning food and 0.6% concerning other products).

In recent years the level of inflation was indicated as a quite low one. For instance, in 2017 the average inflation rate was about 3.67% in comparison to the previous year. In January 2018 the inflation rate was estimated as 2.2%. In May 2018 it was at 2.4% unchanged from the previous month's reading.[8]

§5. Employment Statistics

I. Economically Active Population

47. During the past several years, the number of the economically active population in Russia is estimated as indicated in Table 2.

8. Data by Rosstat www.gks.ru.

Table 2 Economically active population

Year	*Million persons*
2001	71,411
2002	72,421
2005	73,811
2006	74,187
2008	76,000
2011	75,752
2017	72,324.6

48. The employment structure of the economically active population has also been changed with respect to employers' ownership status. For example, from 1992 to 1999 the share of employees decreased from 68.9% to 38.3% in the state and municipal sectors, respectively; at the same time, it increased from 12% to 19.3% in the mixed ownership sector (irrespective of foreign capital participation) and from 18.3% to 41.8% in the private sector. The majority of employment is concentrated in big and medium-size businesses and organizations.

The greatest degree of employment exists in industry. In particular in 2004, the distribution of employees was as follows (in per cent of all employed people):

Sectors	%
Industry	22.1
Agriculture	11.2
Transport	8
Wholesale and trade	16.3
Construction	7.1
Public health and social security	6.8
Education	9.2
Finances, credits and insurance	1.3
Administration	5.3
Other services	12.7

In 2011 the economically active population was distributed in the following way:

Industry	23.2
Construction	7.2
Agriculture	7.9
Trade	17.1

Transport	9.2
Financial and other services	35.6

In 2016 the distribution of economically active population was as follows (in per cent of all employed):

Industry	19.8
Construction	7.2
Agriculture	6.7
Trade	18.5
Transport	9.5
Financial and other services	38.3

Depending on forms of property, in 2006 the distribution of employees was as follows: 33.1% of employees worked in the public sector, whereas 55.4% were involved in the private sector. The same tendency occurs in the recent years.[9]

II. Unemployment

49. Unemployment is still a significant problem in the contemporary Russian labour market. It appeared in 1990 as a consequence of the processes of privatization of big Soviet enterprises and as a result of mass collective redundancies. Russian statistics showed that in 1999 the total number of unemployed reached 8.7 million, or 11% of the economically active population. Concerning that period of time, the ILO estimated Russian unemployment as 8% in 2002, 8.3% in average in 2003 and 8.2% (6.2 million people) at the end of 2004.

50. In 2008 the level of unemployment was accounted as 6.3%, in 2007 as 6.1% and in 2006 as 7.2% of the economically active population.

The economic crisis of 2008 has influenced the employment situation. For instance, in 2009 around 1 million working places in industry were reduced.

51. During recent years, official statistics on unemployment might be estimated as not a dramatic one. According to the official statistics in 2011, the average level of unemployment was 6.6% of the economically active population. In 2016 the unemployment rate was estimated 5.5% (5.7% and 5.3% concerning unemployed male and female, respectively).[10]

52. The difference between rates of registered and real unemployment is one of the characteristics of Russian labour market. According to statistical reports, in

9. *Source*: RF Rosstat – *Russia in Figures. 2006*– Rosstat, Moscow, 2006; *see also*www.gks.ru.
10. Rosstat, *see* www.gks.ru.

April 2002 there were 1.8% registered unemployed (the same figure as in April 2001); in February 2005 the number of officially registered unemployed increased and reached 2.02 million people, or 2.8% of the economically active population. In 2007 of 4.6 million unemployed, 1.6 million were registered at state employment service. In 2009 state employment services registered 3.1 million unemployed (3.8% of the economically active population). In February 2010 the number of registered unemployed has reduced up to 2.3 million people.[11]

53. According to the data provided by the FSLE of the MLSP of the RF in 2017 around 23.1% of unemployed have not had any previous work experience.[12]

Among them 19.8% were students; pupils who were seeking their first job and did not have any professional experience.[13]

54. The employment requirement filed by organizations with the employment service at the end of February 2005 shrank by 70,000 persons from 810,100 in February 2004 and amounted to 740,100 people.[14]

At the end of 2009, the demand for labour reported to the state employment service amounted to 900,000 persons. The number of unemployed population registered at this service, calculated per announced vacancy, amounted to around 2 persons.[15]

55. The average duration of the search for work in past years was in average 8.2 months – 7.8 months for men and 8.8 months for women. The proportion of women among the officially registered unemployed remains high, up to 70%.

56. However there are some reasons for believing that the above figures may be much more dramatic. The problem of the Russian labour market is informal sector, where the legal status of workers involved cannot be defined clearly. *See also* paragraph *60*.

57. Another problem is hidden unemployment, showing itself through non-payments of wages to employees. Over the last decade, this has become a major problem of social policy. For example, according to the data of the Ministry of Statistics of the RF (Goskomstat), at the beginning of 2000, around 10.1% of the total number of employed were put on short-time work, and 11.1% on unpaid (so-called administrative) leave. It is important to note that the current Labour Code (LC) partly solved this problem by introducing more definite means of responsibility of employers for violations in the paying of wages. But the problem of so-called informal employment is still significant in Russia.

---

11. *Ibid.*
12. *Rossiyskaya Gazeta* of 22 Feb. 2005, *see* www.rg.ru.
13. Rosstat, *see* www.gks.ru.
14. Data by the Ministry of Economic Development and Trade. *See* www.economy.gov.ru.
15. RF Rosstat, *see* www.gks.ru.

III. Other Trends in the Labour Market

58. The Russian labour market also has an increasing number of people who have to work under working conditions below the established standards (especially in manufacturing, construction, transport and communications). For example, in 1999, according to Rosstat data, their share in the total workforce was 17.3%. This especially affects migrant workers (from CIS countries and other former Soviet republics).

59. Still enough of migrant workers are ready to work under worse working conditions. As a consequence, the problems of inadequate protection (as regards conditions of employment, occupational safety and health conditions, social security, freedom of association, collective bargaining and access to justice) have acquired particular importance.

60. Conclusion of contracts for work under civil law legislation instead of employment contracts is one of the significant features of Russian market. In this respect it is necessary to note that recent changes to Russian LC has introduced the rule concerning recognition of concluded civil law contracts for works and services which regulate de facto employment relations to be employment contracts.(Article 19.1 of the LC)(*see* paragraphs 81, 82 and 138).

61. It is difficult to determine the exact number of migrant workers, as well as their legal status. The situation is even worse if we take into account that some employers hire migrants illegally and pay them low wages threatening to report them to the authorities. For example, in 2004 the number of migrants working officially were 300,000, whereas the real appropriate figure was estimated around 2 million. In 2017 the rate of migrant workers was estimated as 10% of total working force. Most types of unskilled and unpopular jobs in the construction sector in Moscow are given to migrant workers.[16] At the same time, migration was the main reason for the growth of Russian population in recent years, as well as of violations in the sphere of labour rights of the workers engaged.

62. Moreover, a widespread trend from typical employment to its atypical more flexible forms has appeared in Russia too. For example, temporary employment (which is generally understood as receiving a job through private employment agencies, for a definite time, under a contract with the agency involved) has grown rapidly in the RF during the last decade. In Russia the agency work situations of agency work are usually described as 'leasing of personnel' or, 'rented work'. *See also* paragraph 213.

---

16. *Rossiyskaya Gazeta* of 16 Nov. 2004, *see* www.rg.ru.

IV. The Distinction Between the Private and Public Sectors

63. The ownership structure in Russia has changed considerably. Science, education, a major part of the defence industry, energy, roads, communications, transport and public health have mostly remained the property of the state. Other spheres belong to private or mixed property. In general there are no major differences between public and private sectors as concerns legal regulation of employment. Some particulars will be analysed below; *see also* paragraph 48.

Chapter 2. Definitions and Notions

§1. The Definition and System of LL

64. The LC of the RF contains a definition of LL. This definition is based on a previously used classification of all relations which are regulated by LL into two groups:

(1) employment relationships, which have arisen from a contract of employment; and
(2) so-called close-linked with employment relationships, or other relationships, which are directly associated with employment relationships.

65. It is important to note that the LC (Article 1) lists relationships which are directly associated with employment relationships. In particular, they include relationships in the following spheres:

(a) organization and management of labour;
(b) arrangement of employment at a particular employer (as concerns entering into employment relationship);
(c) professional training and additional professional education of employees directly with a given employer;
(d) social dialogue, which is more often covered by the term 'social partnership' and includes aspects of collective bargaining and concluding collective agreements at different levels;
(e) participation of employees (their representatives) in establishing working conditions and application of labour legislation in cases envisaged in legislation (co-determination);
(f) liability of employers and employees in case of damages of entity (usually called 'material liability');
(g) state monitoring and the control undertaken by trade unions over observation of labour legislation (including legislation on safety at work);
(h) resolving of labour disputes (both individual and collective ones); and
(i) obligatory social insurance in cases, stipulated by federal law.

66. The great majority of scientists do not divide Russian LL into individual and collective law. Under the prevailing theory, the system of Russian LL includes the following parts:

(i) the general part of LL which contains basic notions (the scope and the method of regulation) and principles of Russian LL; sources of LL; general characteristic of all relationships regulated by LL (including the status of participants); social partnership (social bargaining, the role and legal status of collective agreements; and participation of interests of actors of collective bargaining); and

(ii) the particular part of LL which consists of such divisions (legal institutes) as employment contracts; working time; remuneration and work rates; guarantees and compensation; work order and labour discipline; education at work and improving qualification of employees; work and safety; material liability; state monitoring and control over labour legislation and other normative legal acts containing LL rules; defence of labour rights of employees and consideration of labour disputes (both – individual and collective); and peculiarities of regulation of labour of some categories of employees (such as managers of enterprises, teachers and female workers).

67. However, it should be noted that some of the representatives of the science of Russian LL support the idea of its separation into individual and collective LL.[17] Moreover, the style of the current LC may be seen as it takes into account the widespread division of this branch of law into individual and collective parts. Russian LL will be presented in this monograph according to this approach.

§2. The Main Characteristics of Russian LL

68. LL in Russia is an independent branch of law. Russian law is separated into branches by using two main theoretical constructions: the subject of law and the method of regulation.

The subject of a particular branch of law is recognized as the scope of relationships that are regulated by law.

The method of a branch of law is explained through means and instruments (legal acts, contracts, etc.) by which the appropriate relationships are regulated.

I. Employment Relationship

69. The central point of the subject of LL is the employment relationship (also called the 'individual employment relationship') based on the individual contract of employment. Therefore legal rules regulating the procedure of concluding of employment contracts, formation of their content, rights and obligations of the parties; as well as changing and terminating of a contract of employment establish the framework of employment relationship. Such rules may be classified as individual LL in accordance with the classification suggested.

It should be noted that in cases specified by legislation, civil law contracts for works and services may be recognized to be individual employment contracts if they stipulate de facto employment relationships. *See* paragraphs 70 and 138.

70. The prevailing legal theory defines the employment relationship as an engagement in subordinate, dependent work on the basis of the following criteria:

17. Lushnikov, A.M., Lushnikova, M.V., *The Course on Labour Law*, Textbook, Part 1, Moscow: Prospect, 2003, p. 260.

(a) the work undertaken is a broader group of tasks belonging to a type of job (so-called 'labour function' which is defined by profession, specialization and qualification) as distinct from the definite work product or services undertaken by independent contractor;
(b) after concluding the contract of employment, an employee has automatically been included into a collective of workers, and he or she is to a certain extent integrated into the structure of an enterprise. An employer has the right to manage the staff. This power of employer is one of his/her powers in the business sphere (an employer has the economic and organizational authority to decide how the business should be carried out, including the manner of labour utilization). Therefore an employee has an obligation to obey the established regime within an enterprise (internal labour order);
(c) an employee is obliged to follow instructions on the broadest sense (as regards doing not only 'what' but also 'how' and 'when', he may be ordered to use certain instruments or methods, to stop one task and start with another, etc.) whereby he or she becomes subject to the control of the employer. The worker agrees to perform certain work under the authority of an employer, who in turn as a rule provides the necessary machinery, materials and tools;
(d) an employer has to pay the agreed wage: work under an employment contract is remunerated by a regular payment, separate from the business risk of the employer and subject to minimum wage and other LL regulations;
(e) as a rule the work has to be performed on regular, continuous basis; and
(f) an employment relationship is a personal one which means that labour duties must be performed personally, and it is not possible to employ another person as a subcontractor (as distinct from some types of civil law contracts).

Under Russian LL, the main features of the employment relationship derive from the notion of a contract of employment, as well as the legal definition of an individual employment relationship. They are also explained in other chapters of the LC.

II. Individual Contract of Employment

71. Under the LC (Article 56), a contract of employment means an agreement between an employer and an employee stating that the employer is obliged to provide the following:

- work to the employee in accordance with 'labour function'(type of work) as it is specified by the agreement, as well as legal acts;
- guarantees of working conditions envisaged in the labour legislation, collective agreements and local normative acts containing the labour rules; and
- wages to the employee paid in due time and in the appropriate amount.

In turn the employee must fulfil personally the agreed work (in accordance with 'labour function' defined in the contract of employment, as well as in other legal acts) and observe the internal labour rules of the enterprise.

III. Other Relationships Regulated by LL

72. As already mentioned (*see* paragraphs 64 and 65), some other relationships are covered by LL. They occur in connection with an employment relationship which already exists, may be shortly established, or was recently terminated. Among these relationships, for example, are relationships established in the sphere of state monitoring and control which may be undertaken by state services, as well as by trade unions (regarding control). Relationships arising in the sphere of resolving of labour disputes are also regulated by LL. In this respect, it is necessary to note that Russian LL makes a distinction between individual and collective disputes. This distinction is based on differences of subjects, reasons, matters of disputes, etc. As a consequence, there are various procedures for resolving disputes, including participants and the state bodies involved.

73. One of the problems of contemporary LL is whether to include its regulation relationships appearing in the sphere of promotion of employment (in particular, job assistance). The Russian LC makes reference only to job placement with a particular employer (as concerns entering into employment relationship) as being regulated by the LL. At the same time, in practice there are more situations involved in this sphere. Currently they are covered by legislation on promotion of employment and job assistance. The majority of scientists relate this sphere to the LL. But it should be noted that the basic Law No. 1032-1 of 19 April 1991 'On Employment of the Population of the Russian Federation', redrafted in 1996, currently applied with subsequent amendments, most recently in 2018(hereinafter – The Law on Employment), mostly concerns unemployment benefits, while the articles on promotion of employment form a minor part of this law.

IV. Social Partnership and Social Dialogue

74. Labour legislation is widely used both to regulate individual employment relationships and to establish the framework for workers and employers to regulate their relationship through collective patterns of interaction, including collective bargaining.

Social partnership is defined as a system of relations aimed at reaching the balance of interests of employees and employers. It can take the following forms:

- consultations and negotiations on issues concerning regulation of labour relations, provision of guarantees of labour rights of employees, their social protection and improvement of labour legislation;
- regulation of labour relations through collective agreements; and
- participation of employees in management of enterprises.

Employees (their representatives), employers (their representatives), state bodies and local authorities may be involved in social partnership. Russian labour legislation recognizes social partnership as one of its fundamental principles (Article2 of the LC).

75. The notion 'social partnership' is closely connected with the term 'social dialogue', which is not used by Russian law. But mainly the idea of social dialogue is clarified by the term 'social partnership'. Moreover it should be noted that the term 'social dialogue' has been used in the terminology of social sciences and doctrine and is often applied for the purposes of explaining social partnership in publications.

76. Social partnership is mainly realized through the system of concluding collective agreements. The term 'collective agreement' in its narrow sense means a legal act to regulate the social-labour relations between the employer and the employees of an enterprise or individual entrepreneur and its representation by an independent body (Article 40 of the LC).

The existing system of settlement of collective labour disputes is also mostly based on the principles of social partnership.

V. The Method of LL

77. The *method* of regulation is recognized as one of the characteristics of a branch of law. As concerns methods of regulation, LL lies between private and public law. Consequently, methods of contractual regulation and public (centralized) regulation should be coordinated in a proper way.

78. According to labour legislation, the regulation of individual employment relations and other relations, which are directly associated with them, may be implemented by way of concluding, changing and amending of collective agreements, as well as individual contracts of employment. The parties involved enjoy definite degree of freedom. But their freedom is more limited as compared, for example, to civil law (it is explained, in particular, by the thesis that an employee has a weaker position in the labour market that an employer). For example, there is a general rule which requires that neither collective agreements nor individual contracts of employment may contain conditions impairing the level of rights and guarantees of employees specified in the labour legislation. If such conditions are included in the above-mentioned types of contracts, these contracts are not valid.

Besides collective bargaining, Russian labour legislation refers to some spheres of employment which have to be regulated with participation of employees, mainly their representatives (trade unions and so on).

VI. The Principles of LL

79. In general the principles of LL are understood as the main ideas which show the essence of LL norms. It is important to note that the current LC lists the main principles of legal regulation of employment relations and other relations directly linked to them. These are as follows:

(a) freedom of labour, including the right to work which everyone shall freely choose or freely agree to, the right to choose profession and the kind of activities;
(b) prohibition of forced labour and discrimination;
(c) protection against unemployment;
(d) safeguarding the right of every employee to adequate work conditions;
(e) safeguarding the right of every employee to timely and complete payment (equal pay for equal work);
(f) employees' and employers' right of association for protection of their rights and interests, including the right to create trade unions and join them;
(g) guaranteeing of employees to participate in the organization's management in the forms stipulated by law;
(h) combining state and contractual regulation;
(i) social partnership which includes the right of employees, employers and their associations to participate in contractual regulation of employment relations and other relations directly linked to them;
(j) safeguarding the right of employees to protection of their dignity in the framework of their labour activities; etc.

§3. Distinction Between Labour Law and Civil Law

80. As a part of civil law, Russian LL differs from its mother branch of law. LL has been heavily influenced by civil law. At the same time, civil law and its concepts have had no lasting impact.

81. One of the most important aspects of the distinction is that the basic principles of civil law are found in the freedom of a contract, which is restricted in LL. In this respect, it is interesting to note that the problem of the distinction between these two branches of law has become important again since the end of the 1980s. The major recent trend in the past ten years has been the use of civil law contracts instead of employment contracts. This practice has acquired particular popularity in the private sector of economy. One of the reasons behind this tendency was to reduce the level of taxation. The legislation on social security contributions (as well as social taxes), which must be deducted from payments in accordance with the contracts that are regulating work, allowed this possibility. According to this legislation, an enterprise was not obliged to deduct social security contributions from remunerations received by workers under civil law contracts. Of course, there was another reason too: civil law contracts provide more possibilities in the sphere of their termination.

The influence of civil law methods of regulation in the sphere of LL was mainly connected to the processes of establishing the market economy. To reflect these developments, the theory of LL tried to explain the possibilities of incorporating LL into civil law.

82. Nowadays the problem of making a distinction between employment contracts and civil law contracts regulating works and services still has its practical importance. The current CC stipulates the two main types of contracts which regulate providing works and services: a contract for work and a contract for services. Some other contracts (such as commission and agency contracts) may be also taken into consideration in this respect. In practice often it is really difficult to distinguish between employment contracts and civil law contracts. The main distinction is based on the subject of a contract. While an employment contract regulates both the working process and the result, a civil law contract regulates the result of a definite work or a service (Article 702 and Article 779 of the RF CC). Then under civil law contracts, a contractor must independently define ways of fulfilling the customer's assignments, unless otherwise stipulated by an agreement (Part 3, Article 703 of the RF CC). In respect of making distinction between these civil law contracts and an employment contract, it is also necessary to add that tools and materials may be provided if it is stipulated by a civil law contract. But the general rule is that the work must be fulfilled at the contractor's expense: from her materials and with her own means and resources (Part 1, Article 704 of the RF CC). Finally, such contracts may not be concluded for indefinite period. There are also some other differences between civil law contracts and employment, which follow from the principle of freedom of contracts.

§4. Labour Law and Social Security

83. Until the end of 1960s, social security was not considered to be an independent branch of law, or a separate discipline. The appropriate relations (in such spheres as pensions, social insurance of employees and medical help) were regulated by several branches of law (including LL). From the end of 1960s, social security has become an independent branch of Russian (previous Soviet) law.

84. Nowadays the RF Constitution (Article 39) guarantees rights in the sphere of social security for everyone in cases stipulated by law. It establishes the right to health protection and free medical care in national and local medical institutions (Part 1, Article 41 of the RF Constitution); guarantees age-related social security payments in case of illness and invalidity (Part 1, Article 39 of the RF Constitution); and states pensions and allowances (Part 2, Article 39 of the RF Constitution).

85. It should be noted that in previous times, mainly employees enjoyed rights in the sphere of social security. That approach has been changed because of rising unemployment, poverty, etc. Currently an employee is still entitled to the majority of benefits provided by social security. But it is important to note that over the past decades some social security benefits (for instance, paid in the framework of obligatory social insurance schemes) has covered workers as parties to civil law contracts on works and services.

86. The contemporary system of social security is based on classification of all benefits and social services into three main groups: obligatory social insurance; social assistance; and social security of special categories of subjects.

87. The financial system of Russian Social Security is based on social insurance contributions (regulated by different federal laws regarding particular types of obligatory social insurance, as well as the Tax Code). Social insurance contributions are paid only to special social funds which are not included into the state budget. Currently there are three types of such social funds in the RF:

(1) the Pension Fund of the RF (RF PF);
(2) the Social Insurance Fund of the RF (RF SIF); and
(3) the Funds of Obligatory Medical Insurance (FOMI) – including the Federal FOMI and the funds of obligatory medical insurance of the subjects of the RF.

Employers deduct social insurance contributions from wages of employees at sources. The appropriate rates are mostly accounted in accordance with legislation regulating social insurance contributions, as well as the Tax Code. The current rates are defined respectively concerning the types of social insurance (such as pensions, medical insurance and so on). A special regulation exists in respect of benefits and other guaranties in case of professional risks, where the amounts of social contributions are connected to the degree of risks of appropriate types of professional activity. *See* paragraph 94.

88. The main principles of obligatory social insurance are stated by the Federal Law No. 165-FZ of 16 July 1999 'On the Fundamentals of Compulsory Social Insurance' (with amendments and additions, most recently in 2018). In accordance with this law, obligatory social insurance covers such risks as old age; invalidity; temporary disability; maternity; work-related accidents and professional diseases and some others. The particulars regarding the different types of obligatory social insurance derive from legislation (mainly federal laws).

89. The present system of social assistance in Russia is also an integrated part of social security. It aims to help those who are recognized to be in a difficult living situation, as well as to provide protection for socially vulnerable groups. This system of social assistance is regulated by the Federal Law No. 178-FZ of 17 July 1999 'On State Social Assistance' (with subsequent amendments and additions). The main features of the benefits provided in the framework of social assistance are dependency on the average income of persons (families) involved, as well as financing by state budget (as distinct to the social insurance allowances which are financed from the funds mentioned in paragraph 87).

I. Pensions

90. Over the past decade, the pension system in the RF has significantly altered. The transition towards a system of cumulative pensions has taken place within the context of pension reform. On 6 June 2001 the RF President introduced a package of priority federal bills before the State Duma, which were approved conceptually and adopted on first reading by the State Duma on 13 July 2001. They entered into force on 1 January 2002 and were applied with a lot of subsequent amendments.

Currently the pension system of the RF consists of the following levels:

(i) State pensions (so-called basic pensions) are a part of the pension system which ensures the core part of old-age pensions, the core part of the disability pension and the pension to financial dependents whose breadwinner has died, on the basis of allocations from the Federal Budget of public pensions to citizens who cannot work, in accordance with legislation. The system of state pensions also covers military servicemen, policemen, public prosecutors, judges, victims of political repression and other specified groups. Currently it is based on Federal Law No. 166-FZ of 16 December 2001 'On State Pensions in the RF', with subsequent amendments and additions (hereinafter – the Law on State Pensions), as well as on other laws regarding status of specified groups.

(ii) Compulsory (obligatory) pension insurance is the part of the pension system that makes possible the cumulative and insurance element of old-age labour pensions to employees and self-employed through compulsory insurance contributions. It also makes possible the insurance element of pensions to people with disabilities and to financial dependants whose breadwinner has died. This system is based on obligatory insurance contributions which are made to the RF PF. The rates are stated by the legislation.[18]

(iii) Supplementary pension insurance and provisions are the part of the pension system which tops up the state pension and compulsory pension insurance, which provides pensions based on the accumulation of contributions paid by employers and insured individuals into private pension funds. Insured persons are able to choose the pension fund for the purposes of this part of pension insurance.

91. The legislation on obligatory pension insurance also includes the RF Law No. 27-FZ of 1 April 1996 'On Individual Accounts within the System of Obligatory Pension Insurance', as amended most recently in 2016. The law requires that every insured person (mostly employees), as well as employers, responsible for paying the contributions should be registered with regional divisions of the RF PF.

92. Obligatory pension insurance is also regulated by the Federal Law No. 167-FZ of 15 December 2001 'On Obligatory Pension Insurance in the RF', which is applied with amendments.

The legislation makes reference to the following types of pensions:

(1) Old-age pensions which are paid for persons who reached the age of 60 (men) and 55 (women) and have a definite period of employment. The requirements of age may be reduced regarding some categories of registered unemployed people who were employed in the Far North regions, hazardous or dangerous work, etc.[19]

---

18. *See* paras 87 and 91.

19. It should be noted, that new draft of legislation on pensions suggests to increase gradually the actual age for old-age pensions. up to 65 and 60 for men and women respectively.

(2) Disability pensions which are paid in case of invalidity. In order to receive such a pension the insured person should have a minimum of one year of covered employment. But the level of this insurance (e.g., the amount of a pension) depends on age of a person and the reason for disability, as well as on the group (degree) of invalidity.
(3) Survivor pensions which depend on the employment characteristics of the dead person. These pensions are paid to surviving, non-working dependants (including children, a spouse and some other relatives, determined by legislation).

The above-mentioned pensions are related to the previous working activity of receivers (in case of survivor pensions – of the dead person). That is why these pensions are often called 'labour pensions'. If a person did not acquire rights to receive a labour pension, he or she would be covered by state pensions which are providedin accordance with special Federal Law. *See also* paragraph 90.

II. Obligatory Insurance in Case of Industrial Accidents and Occupational Diseases

93. The system of obligatory insurance against professional risks has been dramatically modified in recent years. It is important to note that the appropriate legislation has been in the sphere of social security law. Previously the appropriate guarantees were provided by labour legislation. The right of employees to demand compensation in case of industrial accidents and occupational diseases was established by the Procedures for Compensation by Employers for the Harm Caused on Employees by an Injury, Professional Disease or Other Health Damage Connected with Fulfilment by them of Work Duties (approved by the Decree of the RF Supreme Soviet – the legislative state body of the USSR) in 24 December 1992. It was an obligation of an employer to pay benefits in the cases above.

94. In 1998 the RF 'On Obligatory Social Insurance against Industrial Accidents and Occupational Diseases' was adopted. Consequently, the principles of obligatory social insurance have been applied for professional risk. This system became fully operational from January 2000.

Currently, the system to cover the risk of occupational injury and disease is focused around a system of obligatory social insurance and administered by the RF SIF, which is also responsible for some other social benefits (e.g., sickness and maternity benefits). The Fund's revenue is collected through obligatory insurance contributions. Employers, as well as other subjects concluding some civil law contracts of works and services, are obliged to pay social insurance contributions to the above Fund for the purposes of insurance against professional risks. The rates of such contributions are established by special federal laws regulating tariffs. In accordance with such federal laws, these contributions are differentiated by classes of professional risk. The classes are dependent on groups of industries. Primarily, there were 14 different contribution rates ranging from 0.2% of wages (budgetary sector) to 9.6% of wages (mining). For the year 2001, the number of different tariff rates was increased to 22. Considerable changes in the composition of the risk classes and of the level of the tariffs charged were again implemented recently. Currently the Order of the RF Ministry of Labour of 25 December 2012 is applied in respect of classification of industries.

Now there are 32 contribution rates ranging from 0.2% to 8.5% of all payments to a worker.[20]

95. This sphere of obligatory social insurance covers two types of professional risk: industrial (work-related) accidents and occupational (professional) diseases.

The notion of industrial accident is derived from the LC, which states that the injuries (e.g., those caused by other persons; bites from insects and reptiles; injuries caused by animals; injuries which have occurred as a result of explosions, accidents, destruction of buildings, structures and installations) shall be investigated and registered by an employer as industrial accidents if they happened:

(a) during the working time in the premises of the organization and during the time required to put in order the production tools and clothing prior to or after work; and when working overtime, at weekends or work-free holidays;
(b) when heading for the workplace or coming back using the transport granted by the employer or his/her representative, or in one's vehicle, if the vehicle is used for production purposes by the employer's (or his/her representative's) instruction, or by agreement between the parties to the employment contract;
(c) when going on a business trip or coming back; and
(d) when performing actions, which are not part of the employee's labour duties, but carried out for the employer or his/her representative, or aimed at prevention of an emergency or accident and some others.

The list of occupational diseases is also provided by legislation.

96. The Federal Law 'On Obligatory Social Insurance Against Industrial Accidents and Occupational Diseases' establishes the following types of social benefit:

(a) temporary disability benefit (monthly: in amount of 100% of a wage of a person involved);
(b) monthly allowance in case of invalidity or death of the victim (payment of cash sums to the amount of the wage or its respective part to the victim depending on the degree of professional disability due to this labour injury; in case of death – to dependent members of the family of the person died);
(c) a one-off allowance (the amount of the wage or its respective part, depending on the degree of professional disability due to this labour injury, with taking into account maximal amount defined by Law); and
(d) compensation for additional costs (if any).

20. The RF Law of 22 Dec. 2005 No. 179-FZ, with following amendments.

III. Medical Insurance

97. The RF adopted a nationwide system of obligatory medical insurance in 1993. Currently it covers medical services which are provided directly to patients by public and private health clinics and other medical establishments within the framework of minimum of services listed by the Government (basic programmes of medical services). The scope of these medical services is compulsory for all citizens. Such minimum services include general help, preventive and emergency care, hospitalization, laboratory services, dental care with some exceptions, maternity care, vaccination and transportation. Voluntary medical insurance covers specialized care, expensive medicines and appliances.

Provision of medical services is realized through clinics, hospitals, maternity homes and other medical facilities, including private health providers. But compulsory medical insurance is mostly undertaken through public medical establishments.

The legal base for the medical insurance is the Federal Law No.326-FZ 'On Obligatory Medical Insurance in the RF', adopted in 2010, and applied with following amendments.

98. Compulsory medical insurance is financed from the Federal Fund of Obligatory Medical Insurance of the RF and its regional divisions. Accumulation of this Fund is based on social insurance contributions (social tax), which are paid by all employers. Non-employed persons pay insurance contributions for the purposes of medical insurance in a fixed amount in accordance with a special Law. *See also* paragraph 87.

IV. Family and Maternity Benefits

99. The system of family benefits was strongly modified in 1995 when the Federal Law No. 81-FZ 'On State Allowances for Persons Who Have Children' was adopted. Recently the legislation was supplemented by the RF Law 'On Obligatory Social Insurance in Case of Temporary Disability and in Connection with the Maternity' of 2006, as amended. This legislation provides the range of benefits (such as maternity benefits which are paid during the pregnancy leave of a woman; benefits for the period of the leave for taking care of the child up to the age of 18 months; monthly paid child benefit for educating a child until the age of 16 (in some cases – until 18); and once paid benefit in case of birth of a child). Moreover currently women enjoy the right to receive a definite amount of money ('maternity capital') which may be used, for instance, for the purposes of educating a child.

100. Mostly employees are covered by these benefits. Therefore the amount of maternity benefits which are paid during the pregnancy leave of women is normally accounted as 100% of wages of women.

Some categories of women, who are registered as unemployed after a definite period of working, as well as military servants, also have the right to receive maternity benefits.

101. The family benefit system is mainly based on social insurance principles (except monthly paid benefit for educating a child until the age of 16 (in some cases 18)). The majority of the allowances are financed from the RF SIF. Exception has been made for the monthly paid benefit for educating a child until the age of 16 (18) depending on the level of income of families. It is financed from the state budget. Therefore this benefit is included into the system of social assistance. The amount of this benefit, as well as rules for payment, is established at the level of the RF subjects.

V. Temporary Disability Benefits

102. Temporary disability benefits are issued in case of disease and other damages to health including household injury. Only employees are recognized to be insured against temporary disability. In some cases the benefits are granted for the purposes of taking care of children, as well as other ill family members of insured persons.

The system of these benefits is administered by the RF SIF.

103. The amount of temporary disability benefits is calculated depending on the rate of a wage (in range from 60% to 100% of wage according to length of continuous record of service, number of minor children dependent and other circumstances). The maximum rate of temporary disability benefits is established by law as a fixed sum.[21]

104. The conditions for paying of temporary disability benefit due to injury at work are stipulated by the above-mentioned legislation on industrial accidents and professional diseases (*see* paragraphs 95 and 96).

VI. Unemployment Benefits

105. As mentioned above, social insurance benefits are financed by special social funds. *See* paragraph 87.

Primarily these funds also included the State Employment Fund which was created for the purposes of financing the measures on promoting employment and paying unemployment benefits. But the situation with the State Employment Fund has dramatically changed. Currently unemployment benefits are financed from the state budget. Therefore it is problematic to include the system of unemployment benefits into obligatory social insurance.

106. Unemployment benefits are provided in accordance with the RF Law 'On Employment of Population in the RF'. The benefits cover citizens of economically active age who are registered as unemployed at state employment office (previously

21. The RF Law No. 255-FZ of 29 Dec. 2006, with amendments and agenda, is applied in this respect.

– at the territorial divisions of the MLSP and currently – at the FSLE). Unemployment benefits may also cover dependants of these categories of unemployed.

107. The level of benefits is connected to the previous working activity of receivers. The amount differs from the salaries and the period of receiving. Benefits may be reduced, postponed, suspended or terminated (e.g., if an employee was discharged for violating work discipline – during the time prior unemployment; and violating conditions for job placement or vocational training suggested by state employment service). Benefits are payable equal to 75% of average monthly wage during last two months preceding unemployment for the first three months; 60% for next four months; and 45% for last months. Moreover, there are minimum and maximum amount of allowances which are defined in accordance with the above law.

In general unemployment benefits are paid for twelve months, within eighteen calendar months, up to in total twenty-four months within thirty-six calendar months.

For unemployed persons who do not meet the prior work conditions (to have at least twenty-six weeks of employment during previous year), or have never worked before, the amount of benefits is calculated as a percentage of the minimal unemployment benefit established by the RF Government.

VII. Social Services

108. Russian Social Security also covers social services which are provided for some categories of persons in cases stipulated by legislation. In this respect the RF Law No. 195-FZ of 10 December 1995 (with amendments) 'On Fundamentals of Social Services for the Population of the Russian Federation' should be mentioned. Article 1 of this law envisages social service as a support for daily problems and problems of a socio-medical, psycho-pedagogical and sociolegal nature; and material assistance for the rehabilitation of citizens who have found themselves in a difficult life situation.

§5. Labour Law and Legislation on Public Service

109. The RF Law 'On the State Civil Service of the Russian Federation'[22] has changed the approach concerning the status of public servants. Previously the public service was regulated by the RF Law of 1995 which stated that employment of public servants is undertaken in accordance with labour legislation. The above law introduced another type of a contract to be concluded with a public servant which is recognized as a specific contract as compared to an employment contract. The law also regulates the main aspects of public service: terms of a contract, working time, principles of remuneration and so on.

22. The RF Law No. 79-FZ of 27 Jul. 2004 'On State Civil Service of the Russian Federation', with following amendments, most recently in 2018.

Regarding municipal civil servants, some particulars of legal status are established by the RF Law No. 25-FZ of 2 March 2007 'On Municipal Service in the Russian Federation', which is applied with following amendments.

The legal status of the above-mentioned categories of public servants, as well as of others, has been regulated quite differently as compared to other employees (especially with regard to security of employment and its termination). The status of employees involved in public service is defined by the above legislation regulating this sphere of activity in general.

§6. Concepts Frequently Used by LL

I. The Employee

110. The term 'employee' means a party to a contract of employment concluded under the LL. Currently the definition of employee is included in the LC. According to Article 20 of the LC, an employee is a natural person having initiated employment relationships with the employer. It is important to note that a more precise notion of employee may not be provided without a complex understanding of the nature of the employment relationship, as well as of a contract of employment. For instance, a civil law contract for work or services may be recognized as an employment one in accordance and under the procedure, stipulated by legislation. As a result, the worker engaged acquires a status of employee.

II. The Employer

111. Under Article 20 of the LC, the term 'employer' means a natural person or legal entity (an enterprise or an organization) having initiated an employment relationship with the employee. At the same time, it is also added that other subjects entitled to conclude employment contracts may act as employers, but only if this possibility arises from federal laws.

112. The LC must be observed on the entire territory of the RF by all employers, irrespective of their legal forms and ownership (including subsidiaries of foreign companies, representative offices and branches), as well as by all foreign individuals, companies and international organizations in Russia, unless a specific regulation is applicable pursuant to a federal law or international treaty. Moreover the LC directly covers relations between employed individuals and individual entrepreneurs.

113. Both legal and physical persons may act as employers. At the same time, it should be noted that employment relationship with an employer as a physical person (individual employer) has some specific features as far as labour legislation is concerned.

114. Physical persons may be registered as individual entrepreneurs, in accordance with civil law. A physical person who is not registered as an individual entrepreneur may also act as an employer. Hereinafter such employers will be named as individual employers.

115. Classification of legal persons is based on civil legislation. In accordance with the RF CC (Article 48), a legal person is recognized as an organization which has in its ownership, economic management or operational administration a specific property and fulfils its obligations with this property, may acquire and exercise proprietary and personal non-property in its own name, bear responsibility and be plaintiff and defendant in court.

Legal persons are divided into organizations pursuing profit-making as the main objective of their activity (commercial organizations) or those which do not set profit-making as such an objective and do not distribute derived profits among their partners (non-profit organizations). Commercialorganizations, except unitary enterprises and other types of organizations specified by law, can enjoy civil rights and carry out civil duties that are necessary in order to run any type of activity not prohibited by law. A legal person can engage in some types of activities whose list is specified by law only on receiving a special permit (licence).

Legal persons which are commercial organizations can be created in the form of economic partnerships and companies, production cooperatives and state-owned and municipal unitary enterprises. Legal persons which are non-profit organizations can be created in the form of consumer cooperatives, public or religious organizations (associations), establishments financed by the owner, charitable and other foundations, as well as in other forms provided for by law.

116. The majority of commercial organizations are created in form of joint-stock companies. A joint-stock company is recognized to be a company whose charter capital is divided into a fixed number of shares. Participants in a joint-stock company (shareholders) are not liable for its obligations and run the risk, within the value of shares belonging to them, of losses associated with the company's activity. The legal status of joint-stock companies is also defined by the RF Law 'On Joint-Stock Companies'.[23] The specific legal status of joint-stock companies created by privatizing state-owned and municipal enterprises is also defined by the laws and other legal acts on the privatization of these enterprises.

117. An important role also belongs to unitary enterprises (existed in public sector) among employers. A unitary enterprise is recognized to be a commercial organization which is not conferred the right of property for the property allotted to it by the owner. The property of a unitary enterprise is indivisible and cannot be distributed according to contributions (stocks), including among the employees of the enterprise. Only state-owned and municipal enterprises can be created in the form of unitary enterprises. Regarding the LL it is important to note that there are a lot of special rules and regulations on the work at organizations which are financed by the state budget.

23. The RF Law No. 208-FZ of 26 Dec. 1995, with subsequent amendments and additions.

Chapter 3. Historical Background

§1. Origins

118. Originally labour relations in Russia were regulated by civil law. The individual contract of employment was subject to the general law of contracts. However, the parties' freedom of contract for labour performance had been gradually restricted by state. Over the years, the number of such legislative restrictions has increased.

119. The first steps of creating labour legislation were undertaken in the 1880s. Later on, in 1913 the Charter on Industrial Labour was issued. This Act is recognized as the first one incorporating LL norms. It required that labour relations had to be regulated also by local acts. The latter was understood as legal acts issued by an employer, especially as regarded wages.[24] The science of Russian LL began its history from 1910 onwards. The first attempt to analyse the nature of employment relationship was undertaken by L.S. Tal.[25]

§2. Russian LL during Soviet Times

120. The Soviet model of LL has evolved considerably. Many aspects of labour relations had received their new methods and scope of legal regulation after the October Revolution of 1917. The first legal documents of the Bolshevik Government (the Decrees) restricted forced labour, established equality in the sphere of labour rights and limited the working day to eight hours.

I. The LC of 1918

121. In 1918 the first LC was enforced. But the basic civil law concepts still continued to be applied to issues arising in the labour sphere. At the same time, the above LC envisaged regulation through the use of collective agreements to be developed at enterprise level by the trade unions, in cooperation with enterprise managements.

II. The LC of 1922

122. The next LC was adopted in 1922. It was the period of the beginning of the New Economic Policy. This Code was based on the principles of market economy. It gave the trade unions and their offices at enterprises the right to represent workers

---

24. Lushnikov, A.M., Lushnikova, M.V., *The Course on Labour Law*, Textbook, Part 1, Moscow: 'Prospect', 2003, p. 20.
25. Tal, L.S., *Trudovoi Dogovor: Tsivilisticheskoye Issledovanie/Employment Contract: Civil Law Research*, Yaroslavl, 1913.

and to negotiate collective agreements. A collective agreement was defined as an agreement concluded between a trade union, on the one hand, and the employer, on the other hand, for the purposes of determining conditions of hiring, as well as work conditions at specific enterprises and institutions. The period of the 1920s was also connected to the great development of theory of LL.

123. In the late 1930s, the above LC was changed almost completely. Some of its standards were no longer practically applied although they did survive as parts of the Code (such as the collective bargaining standards), while others were changed dramatically. The role and the scope of state regulation of labour increased radically. Some laws adopted in 1938–1940 established criminal liability for workers for light disciplinary violations. Trade unions had become completely state institutions. Collective agreements were not concluded during the period of 1934–1947.

Agricultural work was not covered by labour legislation. The workers engaged did not enjoy such guarantees as paid annual leave, maternity leave for women and disability benefits.[26]

124. The period of the World War II Russian LL was connected to more active intervention of the state into labour relations. But already in the 1950s, Russian LL had been renovated and changed. The new generation of specialists of LL appeared. The most outstanding representative of that generation was N.G. Alexandrov. His work on theory of employment relationship is recognized as the most important contribution to the science of LL. Moreover he deeply analysed all the essential theoretical problems of LL.

III. The LC of 1971

125. The attempts at economic reform in the 1960s were reflected by labour legislation. In 1967 wages were increased; the duration of annual leave was prolonged, as well as other social guarantees being established. Finally in 1970 the basic legal act for the purposes of the regulation of labour relations at the level of the USSR was adopted.[27] Later on the third LC (as it was called – the Code of Labour Laws) was adopted in 1971. This Code continued to be in force with all its amendments and supplements until the beginning of 2002. The LC of 1971 was designed to encourage the emergence of collective labour in large enterprises and essentially addressed the typical employee of the so-called Fordist model: the employee who worked for a single employer and on the physical premises of that employer, in a full-time job for indefinite period of time. Still, the LC aimed at governing labour relations within a system based on state ownership, mostly managed by means of

26. Lushnikov, A.M., Lushnikova, M.V., *The Course on Labour Law*, Textbook, Part 1, Moscow: 'Prospect', 2003, p. 23.
27. The Fundamentals on Labour Legislation of the Union of Soviet Socialist Republics (USSR) of 15 Jul. 1970.

centralized administrative regulation of employment. For the most part, its standards were of a binding nature; under the law, the status of employees could not be changed by employers either for the worse or for the better.

At that time labour legislation was aimed at keeping the labour force working for the employer. Thus, their standards of employment and, particularly, resignation and dismissal were highly rigid. In most cases dismissal had to be approved by the local trade union.[28]

Collective bargaining and its application were quite formal because the parties were deprived of contractual freedom.

§3. LL Reform in the 1990s

126. The processes of transition (transformation) from planned to market economy in Russia also influenced the nature of labour relations. Disintegration of the central planning of economic development and emergence of new forms of ownership provided objective reasons for radical reforms of labour legislation. The need for changes had been understood as a vital need by all politics, scientists and lawyers. The socio-economic situation demanded a very high degree of flexibility (e.g., in the sphere of dismissal). Such flexibility was practised in many cases without regard for applicable law. The rigid and inflexible nature of labour legislation was among the factors that encouraged the development of the 'shadow' economy. An increasing number of companies used civil law contracts instead of contracts of employment for the purposes of hiring of personnel.

127. The reformation of labour legislation was undertaken in two ways: amending the LC of 1971and adopting new laws on different spheres of LL. The most substantial amendments and supplements to the LC of 1971 were introduced in February 1998 and in September 1992. They reflected not only a new period of economic development, but also the fact that Russia had acquired sovereign statehood with independent legislative system. Mainly they were designed to limit the scope of centralized regulation of labour relations in favour of collective bargaining, and to reduce the number of imperative norms.

128. Regarding adopting new laws within the framework of reformation of labour legislation, the following steps were made. First, the system of guarantees in case of unemployment was established. It should be noted that until 1990, it was not recognized that the problem of unemployment existed in Russia. The RF Law 'On Employment of the Population of the RF' (hereinafter – The Law on Employment)[29] ensures that citizens have the exclusive right to deploy their talents for productive, creative work. The Law on Employment was designed to resolve two major

28. Some changes to this situation could not be regarded as successful ones. For example, in May 1986, a standard was introduced permitting termination of employment on the grounds that the employee had reached retirement age. This standard was declared unconstitutional by the RF Constitutional Court in February 1992 and repealed on 12 Mar. 1992.

29. The RF Law No. 1032-1 of 19 Apr. 1991, with subsequent amendments and additions.

problems – to prevent excessive lay-offs and to provide social protection to the unemployed. As far as the protection of the unemployed is concerned, the law stipulates necessary conditions for their official recognition and payment of benefits. The above law also defines the status of state employment service; and the range of rights of persons in the sphere of employment (to work abroad, to search for job through state employment service or private employment agencies, to be registered as unemployed and so on).

129. Radical changes in ownership relations, and the increased independence of employees' organizations from the state and from employers, were some of the objective preconditions for the development of a system of social partnership, aimed at achieving an optimum balance between the interests of employees, employers and society as a whole. In many respects, the legal base for social partnership in Russia has been formed under the influence of norms and rules developed by the international community, first of all by those defined by the ILO Conventions and Recommendations on the promotion of collective bargaining and freedom of association.

The term 'social partnership' (which is mostly used in Russia instead of a widespread notion 'social dialogue') appeared in the Presidential Decree of 15 November 1991 'On Social Partnership and Settlement of Labour Disputes'. It was found advisable to enter into tripartite industry-wide agreements between executive authority bodies, trade unions and owners (employers) that would envisage, among other things, observing the workers' interests in the course of privatization. In 1992 the RF Law 'On Collective Agreements' was adopted. The law regulated collective bargaining procedures, rights and obligations of the parties involved, standard contents of collective agreements and some other aspects. It has to be noted that the above law introduced a new concept of a collective agreement, as well as it defined the types of agreements of various levels. For the purposes of developing social dialogue, the Russian Tripartite Commission on Regulation of Social and Labour Relations (RTC) was established. Its status was defined by amendments introduced into the Law 'On Collective Agreements' in 1995. Since 1 May 1999 the activities of the Commission have been regulated by the federal law.[30] The RTC was entrusted with concluding the General Agreement (the highest level of collective agreements) and settlement of labour disputes. The Commission Secretariat received the status equal to the status of the Government Office. During that period the Commission often considered applications of employers' associations and trade unions. Most such applications concerned disagreements encountered while concluding collective agreements. *See also* paragraphs 160,504 and 505.

130. In the 1990s many new trade unions appeared. The most important trade union – the Federal Independent Trade-Union Organization (FNPR) – was established to be really independent from traditional Soviet trade unions. The USSR Law 'On Trade Unions, Their Rights and Guarantees of Their Activity' of 10 December

30. RF Law No. 92 'On Russian Tripartite Commission for Regulation of Social and Labour Relations' of 1 May 1999.

1990 provided a legal framework for the existence of trade union pluralism. Later their status was defined by Russian federal legislation.[31]

131. Strikes and other collective actions of employees caused the need to resolve a number of issues related to collective bargaining, primarily to create a legal framework for the settlement of labour disputes. In response to the mineworkers' strikes of the summer of 1989, the USSR Law 'On Collective Labour Disputes' was enacted on 9 October 1989.[32] For the first time, since the LC of 1922 Russian legislation recognized workers' right to strike.

132. The system of resolving of collective disputes have been also received its legal framework at the level of the RF. By the Governmental Order 304-p dated of 16 February 1992, the Ministry of Labour was instructed to finalize, within one week, establishing services for resolving labour disputes at ministerial and local levels. It was considered expedient to form territorial tripartite commissions for regulation of social and labour relations and to delegate to them the issues on social protection of citizens and provision of employment for population. Later the RF Law 'On Settlement of Collective Disputes'[33] have been passed, and as a consequence changes and amendments to the LC were introduced.

133. The system of compensation in case of industrial accidents and professional diseases was dramatically modified. First, these legal rules shifted in the sphere of social security law. Previously the above guarantees were provided within labour legislation. Since the FR Law No. 125-FZ 'On Obligatory Social Insurance against Industrial Accidents and Occupational Diseases'[34] came into force (in 2000), the principles of social insurance have been applied for such situations. The current LC contains only a definition of industrial accidents, as well as the procedure for investigating them.

§4. The Current LC

134. Despite the fact that Russian labour legislation had been considerably updated, in many respects it still needed to be developed. In particular, it remained focused on the economic model under which the state, setting the rules for regulation of labour relations, as well as guarantees and privileges, was responsible for their financing and implementation. The legislation was recognized as being overburdened with guarantees and privileges absolutely impractical under existing economic conditions. In many instances, lack of the machinery to put labour rules into practice and to establish a strict control over their observance brought about wider

31. *See also* paras 465, 466 and 478–481.
32. The current procedure of collective labour disputes settlement is established by the RF Labour Code (LC).
33. Federal Law of the RF 'On Procedure of Settlement of Collective Labour Disputes' No. 175-FZ of 23 Nov. 1995 (hereafter – The Law on Settlement of Collective Disputes).
34. Federal Law No. 125-FZ of 24 Jul. 1998 'On Obligatory Social Insurance against Industrial Accidents and Occupational Diseases', with subsequent amendments and additions.

legal nihilism. To a certain extent, labour legislation did not cover numerous groups of workers employed by small businesses and physical persons, as well as part-time and seasonal workers. Civil law contracts were still concluded instead of employment contracts. At the same time, an interpretation of the law in force sometimes required invoking sets of civil law provisions. For example, the distinction between an employment contract and a contract for services concluded under civil law (which was often concluded instead of a contract of employment) was mostly based on provisions of the CC. Moreover the provisions of the LC of 1971 did not prescribe any exact procedure for recognizing an employment contract to be void. At the same time, a number of normative acts refer labour relations to the sphere of civil legislation, even though they possess all the features of labour legislation. Due to the lack of clear definition of the subject of LL in the labour legislation, many difficulties occurred when determining to which branches of the law agreements belong, and first of all at consideration of labour disputes in judicial order. As a result, under new economic conditions, the balance of economic interests of employees and employers and their legal rights has been disturbed. An employer has acquired an obvious advantage over employee who was subordinate to him.

135. Relations between legislation of federal level and the level of the subjects of the RF had not been clearly determined. For example, the Republic of Bashkortostan has adopted its own LC. When regulating the labour relations in the Republic, the Republican Code is applied rather than the Federal Code. And many experts pointed out that the Republican Code contained norms contradicting the federal legislation.

136. All the above strongly demanded more dramatic changes of labour legislation. Further ways to reform labour legislation were widely discussed. Several (about thirty) drafts of new LC were introduced in the State Duma of the RF.

Finally on 30 December 2001, the RF President signed Federal Law No. 197-FZ 'On Adopting of the Labour Code of the Russian Federation'. The new LC entered into force on 1 February 2002. The new LC revised existing labour legislation, replacing the previous Code that has been in force for more than thirty years. The new LC was seen as a compromise between different participants of the process of regulation of employment relations (such as employers, trade unions, and state bodies). The new LC has incorporated some previously adopted laws (e.g., the RF Law 'On Settlement of Collective Disputes' and the RF Law 'On Collective Agreements'). Although the new LC retained many of the provisions from previous labour legislation, there were a number of significant changes. In particular, it contains the following new provisions:

- a clear distinction between labour and civil law;
- rules regarding sharing of competences of federal state bodies and the bodies of the subjects of the RF;
- the priority of the LC over other laws and legal acts containing the norms of LL;
- a broader sphere of contractual regulation of labour relations (especially as concerns changing and termination of employment, as well as collective bargaining);

- a broader range of mandatory provisions that need to be included into an employment contract;
- the rule according which the minimum wage cannot be lower than the minimum cost of living established by law (previously, it could not be lower than the minimum monthly wage);
- more detailed responsibility of employers in case of delayed wages; and
- new requirements in the sphere of employees' personal data protection.

137. After the adoption of new LC, amendments to it were introduced several times. In particular, the main idea of the first amendment (introduced on 24 July 2002) was to grant disabled employees an opportunity to be employed for night jobs (in case of their consent in writing). The original text of the RF LC (Part 5, Article 96) totally prohibited hiring the disabled for night jobs.

138. Considerable changes were introduced into Part VI of the RF LC concerning remuneration of labour, in particular a minimum wage. *See* paragraphs 323–325.

Some changes appeared as regards minimum rates for salaries for employees of budget-financed organizations. Significant new rules were added into the mechanism offering guarantees and compensation for those in shift work (Article 302 of the RF LC). It is also necessary to mention the changes into the legal regulation of labour of the persons working and living in the regions of the Far North and areas equated with them (and corresponding amendments into RF Law 'On State Guarantees and Allowances for Those Working and Living in the Far North and Comparable Regions' and into the RF LC). In particular it was stated that guarantees and allowances for this categories of employees are established at different levels, depending on sources for financing of employers (Federal Budget; budgets of the subjects of the RF; and municipal budgets).

The RF Federal Law No. 90-FZ of 30 June 2006 has amended and changed a great number of articles of current LC. They covered approximately all of chapters of the LC. They are referred to below in more detail.

In 2008 the current LC was enriched by a new chapter containing the main principles regulating the labour of sportsmen.

Some new rules and regulations (e.g., connected to safety at work) were added to the LC in 2009 (Articles. 223 and 230).

Recent important changes to the RF LC were introduced in 2012. In particular, the notion of disciplinary sanction has been corrected (Article 192), some aspects of employment of leaders in the sphere of public service have been detailed (Article 349.1), some features of collective negotiations have been renewed and so on.

Among last changes to labour legislation, the ones of 2016 and of 2018 have acquired a special importance. In particular the rule concerning recognition of concluded civil law contracts for works and services, which regulate de facto employment relations to be employment contracts. The LC was enriched by the rules of recognition of such contracts as employment ones. In case of doubts in respect of legal status of workers engaged, the decision is made in favour of employment relationship (Article 19.1 of the LC). This rule was proved and interpreted by the legal practice of the RF Supreme Court in its practical guidelines on application of labour legislation.

From the year 2014, the particulars of regulating of agency work (as regards the legal status of temporary employees hired through personnel agencies) are prescribed by the RF LC (Chapter 53.1). *See* paragraph 213.

Since 2014 the RF LC has regulated the particulars of hiring of foreign employees as well as stateless citizens in the separated Chapter 50.1. *See* paragraphs 200 and 201.

Chapter 4. The Role of Government Institutions in the Shaping and Administering of Labour and Industrial Relations Policy

§1. General Remarks

139. Radical transformations in the adoption of a market economy have reduced the scope of state regulation of labour relations in Russia. At the same time, privatization in many spheres has increased the independence of employees' organizations from the state and from employers. In this respect the main role of the state in the contemporary Russian economic situation is to provide the legislative framework for labour relations.

The legislative regulation of the individual employment relationship typically entails the enactment of legislative provisions governing the formation and termination of contracts of employment, rights and obligations of the parties, also other different aspects – minimum age for employment, protection of young workers, equality at work, hours of work, paid holidays, payment of wages, occupational safety and health and maternity protection. The intervention of the Russian state into labour relations is felt most heavily in the field of regulation of budget-financed organizations. Mainly these are state universities, colleges, state medical institutions and so on.

§2. Government Departments and Services

I. The Ministry of Labour and Social Protection

140. Until 2004 the Ministry of Labour and Social Development of the RF (MLSD) was the main government body as far as the shaping and administering LL and social security were concerned. Administrative reform carried out by the RF President over the past few years has brought some important changes in the sphere of managing of labour. In particular the former MLSD has been restructured as the MHC and Social Development of the RF (MHSD) – nowadays the MLSP.[35]

141. The currently functioning MLSP includes the departments which are responsible for certain areas. In particular, as regards labour relations, it is necessary to mention the following departments of the MLSP: the Federal Agency of Healthcare and Social Development; the Federal Service for Supervision in the Area of Healthcare and Social Development; and the FSLE.

---

35. The Decision of the Government of the RF Law No. 153 of 6 Apr. 2004 'On Issues of the Ministry of Public Health and Social Development of the Russian Federation' (with amendments and additions of 12 Oct. 2007); the Decision of the Government of the RF Law No. 252 of 27 May 2004 'On Certain Issues of the Organization of the Activity of the Federal Service for Supervision in the Area of Public Health and Social Development, the Federal Labour and Employment Service, and the Federal Agency of Public Health and Social Development' (with subsequent amendments and additions).

II. The Federal Service on Labour and Employment

142. It should be noted that mostly the FSLE is competent to regulate labour relations, as well as to issue the appropriate legal acts in this sphere. The legal status of the FSLE is defined by the Regulation of the Government of the RF No. 156 of 6 April 2004 'On Jurisdiction of the Federal Service on Labour and Employment'.[36] It is a federal executive body responsible for employment and alternative non-military service, as well as executive functions of control and supervision of observance of labour legislation. The FSLE also executes functions of rendering state services in the spheres of promotion of employment and protection against unemployment, labour migration and settlement of collective labour disputes.

§3. State Monitoring and Control

143. State monitoring and control in the sphere of labour legislation is realized by several state bodies. It should be noted that the competence of control is also vested in trade unions.

144. The main controlling state body in the RF is the office of public prosecutor. On behalf of the state, this office carries out the supervision of execution of all laws and observance of rights and freedoms of the person and the citizen. The General Prosecutor of the RF is appointed to the post and is dismissed by the Federation Council on the representation of the President of Russia. The basic law on regulating the competence of prosecution is the RF Law of 2 April 2014, with following amendments.

145. The current RF LC reflects the distribution of functions of state supervisory and controlling bodies in the area of labour. The LC makes reference to the following main groups of such federal bodies:

(1) the State Labour Inspection which was created for the purposes of control in the sphere of observing labour legislation.[37] Currently the legal status and competence of State Labour Inspectors is defined by the RF LC which contains a special chapter regulating state monitoring and control;
(2) special state bodies which are responsible for state supervision and control along with State Labour Inspection. Mostly they are competent to undertake state monitoring and control in specific branches and certain spheres of industry.

36. The Decision of the Government of the RF Law No. 324 of 30 Jun. 2004 'On Endorsing the Regulations on the Federal Labour and Employment Service', with additions and amendments.
37. The Decree of the President of the RF Law No. 850 of 4 May 1994 'On State Supervision and Control Over the Observance of Labour Legislation and Legislation on Labour Protection of the Russian Federation'.

146. The Federal State Labour Inspection is under the jurisdiction of the MLSP (in particular, of the FSLE). It has the function of implementing state supervision and control over enforcement of legislation of the RF on labour and occupational safety.

The Chief State Inspector of Labour of the RF is appointed to and released from his duties by the Government of the RF.

The RF Government's Decision No. 875 of 1 September 2012 regulates the status and competence of The Federal State Labour Inspection in more detail.

147. As executives of the State Labour Inspection, State Labour Inspectors are appointed to and relieved from their office by the Chief State Inspector of Labour of the RF. In carrying out monitoring and control, State Labour Inspectors are entitled to the following activities:

(a) to visit employers (organizations of all forms of ownership, as well as employers – physical persons);
(b) to request documents, explanations and information needed to fulfil state monitoring and control;
(c) to investigate, in accordance with the established procedure, industrial accidents with the view to establishing the reasons and developing recommendations to prevent their future occurrence;
(d) to present employers (their representatives) with obligatory instructions to eliminate violations of labour legislation; and
(e) to handle cases of administrative offences (as regards violations of labour legislation) in accordance with the established procedure and their competence and so on.

As mentioned above, State Labour Inspectors are empowered to hear cases of violations of labour legislation, as well as other legal acts containing LL standards. In this sphere they may act only within their competence and in accordance with the defined legal procedure. The sanctions, as well as the appropriate procedures are established by the RF Code of Administrative Offences.

State Labour Inspectors are required to preserve legally protected secrets (state, official, commercial) that become known to them while exercising their powers (Article 358 of the LC). Decisions of State Labour Inspectors may be appealed to the Chief State Labour Inspector of the RF, and/or to the court of general jurisdiction (Article 361 of the LC).

It should be noted that some changes to the RF LC have corrected some rights and duties of State Labour Inspectors. In particular, they have been vested with the right to visit all employers for the purposes of inspecting. This concerns not only organizations, but also employers who are physical persons.

148. State monitoring in special industries is vested in state executive bodies (their divisions) which are responsible for the appropriate sphere of economy. The

RF LC makes reference to state monitoring of measures enacted to ensure safe servicing of electric and heating installations –energy control (Article 367 of the RF LC), state public health and epidemiological monitoring (Article 368 of the RF LC) and some other functions.

For monitoring in the sphere of labour migration *see* paragraph 155.

§4. Promotion of Employment

149. One of the priorities of state employment policy is to assist the population in finding work. Mostly the state policy on employment promotion is defined by the RF Law on Employment. Some aspects in this sphere are also regulated by legislation adopted at the level of subjects of RF. *See also* paragraph 128.

150. There are two types of employment intermediaries in Russia – territorial agencies of public employment service and private employment (recruitment) agencies.

151. In 1991 the Federal State Employment Service was established as an independent state body. It consisted of departments in the subjects of the RF and more than 2,600 state-run job centres in regions. Later on the State Employment Service was reorganized and included into the system of the previous MLSD (currently it is represented by FSLE of the MLSP).

In accordance with the RF Law on Employment, the main task of this service was to give free assistance to citizens looking for work. It is also responsible for providing consultations for professional guidance; professional training of the unemployed; allocation to posts by quota; assistance in setting up small businesses and working as a self-employed person. With the help of this service, in 2005 around 4,075,800 unemployed people found paid work, and 1,828,900 of them did not have any previous working experience. In 2016 around 64.4% of registered unemployed have found work with assistance of state employment service. [38]

152. The Russian state supports private employment (recruitment) agencies, mainly by participating in providing the legal framework for their activity, as well as by licensing their activity. The market of private employment agencies has evolved successfully in Russia. For instance, in Moscow alone 250 recruiting agencies were registered in 2005. By June 2017 around 665 private employment agencies had been registered in the RF. Currently such agencies function effectively, also by using well-known means of new forms of employment and services (e.g., executive search, human resources consulting, out stuffing and job assistance). *See also* paragraph 213.

---

38. Source: RF Rosstat – '*Russia in Figures. 2006*' – Rosstat, Moscow, 2006; www.gks.ru.

§5. Vocational Training

153. For the purposes of promotion of employment, Russia has a state system of vocational training and psychological support for the population. It includes territorial centres which offer vocational guidance and psychological support to young people, as well as subdivisions of the public employment service which offer vocational guidance and psychological support to the population of the RF. Apart from these services, educational psychologists and professional consultants give vocational guidance to young people in the education system. Psychologists and experts on the social and professional rehabilitation of disabled people offer vocational guidance to invalids. Access to vocational guidance is available to anyone who wants it throughout the whole territory of the RF.

154. The system for training the unemployed and members of the population without gainful employment is constantly developing and improving. More than 1.8 million unemployed people were sent for professional training by the employment service during the period 1991–2000. In 2000 alone, more than 2,153,000 unemployed young people were assisted with professional education.

The effectiveness of vocational training for the unemployed is constantly growing. In 1991 67% of the total of unemployed who were retrained found work, in 1996 it was 75.3%, in 1997 86%, and in 2000 it was 93.1%.

§6. The Admission of Foreign Employees

155. The Russian state is very active in regulating the processes of admission of foreign workers. The appropriate legal framework was created in 1993, when the Decree of the President of the RF No. 2146 'On Recruitment and Employment of Foreign Manpower in the RF' of 16 December 1993 was adopted. Currently the admission of foreign employees, as well as the procedure thereof, are regulated by the RF Law on Legal Status of Foreign Citizens in the RF No. 115-FZ of 25 July 2002, with subsequent amendments, most recently in 2018. Currently the RF LC has a new chapter, which regulates particulars of hiring of foreign personnel.

According to the legislation, Russian citizens have priority rights in filling vacant workplaces. Employers receive permits for recruitment of foreign employees. They are also obliged to pay a charge for each recruited foreign worker. At the same time, foreign employees should receive confirmation to perform work on the territory of the RF. Employers recruiting foreign manpower without a due permit are held liable under RF legislation (in particular, under the RF Code of Administrative Offences). The above procedure is not applied to certain categories of workers (e.g., employees of international organizations). There are also restrictions on hiring foreign workers in some spheres of labour activity (in particular, foreign citizens do not have the right to be engaged in state or municipal service). Foreign employees (labour migrants) must be registered by the Federal Migration Service (acting under the jurisdiction of the Ministry of Internal Affairs of the RF) in accordance with the legislation (the RF Law of 18 July 2006 No. 109-FZ 'On Migration Account of Foreign Citizens and Persons Without Citizenship').

In regulating the processes of labour migration, the Russian state provides quotas for foreign workers. For example, in 2018 Russian Government established quotas for labour migrants at 178, 752 invitations for the purposes of labour activity.

It should be noted that the number of migrants is steadily growing in Russia, mostly because of ones from the CIS countries (e.g., Azerbaijan, Armenia and Moldova). For instance, in 2010 the degree of foreign workers from CIS countries was accounted as 76% of total number of labour migrants in Russia.

156. The above topic is also regulated at the level of subjects of the RF. For instance, as regards Moscow, the Law of the city of Moscow 'On Registration of Foreign Labour in Moscow' was adopted on 19 September 2001. It is focused on protection of rights and lawful interests of citizens of the RF living in Moscow by the registration of foreign citizens and persons without citizenship in the labour market. This registration is carried out with the aim of revealing migration processes to Moscow and formulating a rational migration policy. Labour activity is understood in the law rather widely: it is not only work on the basis of employment contract, but also any other activity carried out by a person and bringing him/her income. The law prescribes the application of a permissive procedure for employment and employer use of the foreign labour force in Moscow. *See also* paragraphs 200–202.

157. Recruitment and use in the RF of foreign manpower are effected taking due account of the opinion of All-Russia Associations of Trade Unions or territorial associations of trade union organizations. *See also* paragraphs 472–478.

§7. Russian State and Collective Bargaining

158. The Russian state provides conditions for collective bargaining, typically without any direct interference into the bargaining process (except for situations when it acts as an employer or when the economic situation becomes difficult). In principle workers and employers can negotiate freely, but within the framework of the Constitution and laws. At the same time, when analysing the role of the state in collective bargaining, some legislative limitations should be taken into account. In particular, this concerns the principle of prohibition of acts hindering the conclusion, revision or application of collective agreements. According to this principle, state bodies, as well as political parties and any association of employers, are prohibited from intervening in any manner whatsoever with a view to restricting the legal rights of workers or their representatives in the conclusion, revision or application of collective agreements.

159. The Russian Government participates in tripartite mechanisms as usual forms of social partnership (social dialogue). First, the state may be one of the social partners (in accordance with the LC, the state may be represented by the Government and the local executive power bodies, as a party to the collective bargaining process). Second, the state takes part in the supervision of the application of collective agreements. Such supervision is carried out directly by the parties or their empowered representatives, as well as the state bodies involved. Finally, the state acts, whenever necessary, as an employer.

160. The process of creating the system of collective bargaining of the RF was connected with the establishing of the RTC as a permanent body. The status of the RTC is currently defined by the LC (Article 35) and the RF Law 'On Russian Tripartite Commission for Regulation of Social and Labour Relations' of 1 May 1999 N92-FZ. The main functions of the above commission are to carry out collective bargaining and to elaborate draft General Agreements. Among its other functions are promotion of the regulation of social and labour relations at federal level; carrying out consultations on issues related to the elaboration of draft federal laws and other normative acts of the RF on social and labour relations, etc. *See also* paragraphs 504 and 505.

Chapter 5. Sources of LL

§1. General Remarks

161. The sources of Russian LL may be classified by legal force, as well by the sphere of application. By legal force the sources of LL are divided into laws of the highest legal force (the Constitution; federal constitutional laws; federal laws; laws of subjects of the RF) and sub-legal acts (Decrees of the President of the RF; Orders of the Government, branch orders, instructions, rules of ministries and departments, legal acts of local administrations). By the sphere of application, the sources of LL are classified as federal, branch (subjects of the RF) and local. They also depend on the range of persons covered.

162. Article 11 of the LC defines the sphere of LL. In particular, labour legislation applies to all employees (persons who entered contracts of employment) in the whole territory of the RF for all employers (legal entities or natural persons) regardless of their organizational forms and types of ownership. Changes to the RF LC of 2006 have stressed that labour legislation, as well as secondary normative acts containing LL rules, are also applied to other relationships on using of personal labour if this is prescribed by the LC or other federal laws (Article 11 of the RF LC).

The laws and other normative legal acts of the subjects of the RF containing LL rules are applied within the territory of the appropriate subject of the RF.

It has to be noted that on the territory of the RF, labour legislation covers all employment relations of foreign citizens, stateless persons, organizations created or founded by them or with their participation, employees of international organizations and foreign legal entities, if otherwise it is not envisaged in the federal law or international treaty of the RF.

163. Labour legislation is not applied to the following persons (if they do not act simultaneously as employers or their representatives according to the procedures established in the LC):

- servicemen of military service when they execute the duties of the military service;
- members of the boards of directors (supervisory boards) of organizations (except for the persons having concluded an employment contract with the given organization);
- workers under civil law contracts for works and services, as long these contracts are not recognized to be employment ones in accordance to the legislation (*See* paragraph 138); and
- other persons if this is established in the federal law.

Military service is not included in the sphere of LL. The RF LC makes reference only to persons who have concluded contracts of employment with military bodies, establishments, military higher and secondary professional training and educational institutions, as well as persons undergoing an alternative civil service in place of the military. Such persons are subject to regulating factors, provided by the RF LC.

164. In accordance with the Decree of the Supreme Soviet of the RF 'On Ratification of the Agreement on Establishing the Commonwealth of Independent States' of 12 December 1991, legislation of the Soviet Union concerning labour relations continues to be in force in the part which does not contradict the relevant legislation of the RF.

§2. The RF Constitution

165. The Constitution of the RF has the greatest legal power (*see also* paragraphs 186 and 187). It proclaims the RF to be a social state whose policies are aimed at creating conditions which ensure a dignified life and free development of the person. It also makes a reference to the main principles of legal regulation of the social sphere. In particular, these are as follows:

(i) Free movement of services within the territory of the RF is provided. Restrictions may be established by the federal law, if this is necessary for the protection of the people's safety, their lives and health and protection of environment and cultural values (Article 74 of the RF Constitution).
(ii) Any forms of discrimination are prohibited. The RF Constitution guarantees the equality of rights and liberties regardless of sex, race, nationality, language, origin, property or employment status, residence, attitude to religion, convictions, membership of public associations or any other circumstance. Any restriction of the rights of citizens on social, racial, national, linguistic or religious grounds is forbidden. Men and women have equal rights and liberties and equal opportunities for their pursuit.
(iii) Special protection of vulnerable groups is guaranteed. Article 38 of the RF Constitution contains legal grounds for peculiarities of the status of female and young workers in employment. Motherhood, childhood and the family are under state protection. *See also* paragraph 425.

166. Article 37 of the Constitution contains the list of basic labour rights, including free choice of type of activity and profession, working conditions which meet safety and hygiene requirements, remuneration without any discrimination, minimum wage established by federal law, protection against unemployment, right to individual and collective labour disputes, right to strike, guaranteed statutory duration of work time, days off and holidays and paid annual vacation. Article 30 envisages that everyone shall have the right to association, including the right to create trade unions in order to protect their interests.

167. Taking into account the federal structure of the RF, it is also necessary to add that the RF Constitution refers labour legislation to the joint jurisdiction of the

RF and its subjects, which implies the supremacy of federal legislation over the legislation of the subjects of the Federation where contradictions occur. The subjects of the Federation, however, are empowered to raise, at their own expense, the level of labour rights and social guarantees in relation to the level set by the federal authorities. They have the right to make the rules set at the federal level more detailed and specific and to supplement them for the purpose of improving the well-being of workers and citizens and to adopt acts concerning problems that have not been resolved by the federal legislation.

§3. Federal Laws

168. In the theory of Russian law, the term 'legislation' is used from two point of views. In a narrow sense, legislation means all legal acts (mostly laws) which are adopted by legislative bodies (at the federal level – by the Federal Assembly of the RF). In a broader sense, the notion 'legislation' covers all normative legal acts adopted not only by the Parliament, but also by other state bodies (both at federal level and at the level of subjects of the RF). From this point of view, labour legislation also includes such legal acts as Decrees of the RF President, Orders or Decisions of the Government, legal acts of federal ministries and departments, as well as appropriate legal acts issued at the level of the subjects of the RF. In this monograph, the term 'legislation' will be understood in a broader sense. In this respect the laws adopted by the RF Parliament will be referred to as RF laws, or federal laws.

169. Following the Russian LC, the sources of labour legislation also include constitutions (charters), laws and other normative legal acts of the subjects of the RF, as well as acts of the bodies of self-local government and local normative acts containing the norms of labour legislation. The latter is created at the level of a particular employer in accordance with the established rules.

I. Federal Constitutional Laws

170. The highest level of laws is represented by federal constitutional laws which are characterized by a special procedure for adoption. The RF Constitution makes reference to the spheres which are regulated by federal constitutional laws. Mostly the status of state bodies (such as the Government, the Federal Supreme Courts and so on) is determined by this kind of law.

II. Federal Laws

171. Federal laws are adopted by the Parliament of the RF – Federal Assembly. *See also* paragraphs 9, 10, 187 and 188.

172. Among federal laws the LC has the most important position (*see also* paragraph 188). The current LC was signed in 2001, and it has been in force since 1 February 2002. Since its adoption the RF LC has been amended several times. The LC is regularly amended. For instance, important changes have been introduced in the years 2006, 2014 and 2017.

Among the laws as sources of LL the LC has priority. It has binding force for all types of employer.

The LC consists of sixty-two chapters which deal, *inter alia*, with the following major LL issues:

(a) Fundamentals of labour legislation (purposes of labour legislation; basic principles of regulation; non-discrimination; prohibition of forced labour; and the system of labour legislation);
(b) the respective competencies in LL making of the RF and of its subjects;
(c) characteristics of employment relations (including employee's and employer's basic rights and responsibilities);
(d) social partnership, including tripartite cooperation, collective bargaining and workers' participation;
(e) contracts of employment;
(f) protection of workers' personal data;
(g) conditions of work, including work time; rest time, including leave; and remuneration;
(h) labour discipline;
(i) health and safety;
(j) women's labour, including maternity protection;
(k) youth (under 18 years of age) labour;
(l) seasonal work, home work, domestic work, agency work, etc.;
(m) work in a number of specific sectors, including education and transportation; and hiring of foreign employees;
(n) protection of workers' rights by trade unions; and
(o) labour dispute settlement.

173. Labour legislation is also represented by other federal laws. Among them the following ones acquire the particular importance:

- the RF Law No. 1032-1 'On Employment of the Population of the Russian Federation' of 19 April 1991, with amendments and additions (hereinafter The RF Law On Employment);
- the RF Law No. 92 'On Russian Tripartite Commission for Regulation of Social and Labour Relations' of 1 May 1999;
- the RF Law No. 156-FZ On Employers' Associations' of 27 November 2002, with amendments and additions;
- the RF Law No. 10-FZ 'On Trade Unions, Their Rights and Guaranties of Performing the Activity' of 12 January 1996, with amendments and additions (hereinafter – the RF Law On Trade Unions);

- the RF Law No. 134-FZ 'On the Minimum of Subsistence in the Russian Federation' of 24 October 1997 (with subsequent amendments and additions); and
- the RF Law No. 4520-1 'On State Guarantees and Compensations to Persons Working and Living in the Regions of the Far North and the Districts being Equal thereto' of 19 February 1993 (with subsequent additions and amendments) and some others.

174. Federal laws are officially published. Unpublished laws are not applicable. No regulatory legal act affecting the rights, liberties or duties of the human being and citizen may apply unless it has been published officially for general knowledge. The official sources for publication of Russian Federal Laws are *Rossiyskaya Gazeta*, as well as the Law Book (*Sobraniye Zakonodatel'stva*) of the RF, or the newspaper of the RF Parliament (*Parlamentskaya Gazeta*).

§4. Decrees of the President of the RF

175. The President of the RF issues Decrees and executive orders, which are binding throughout the territory of the RF and may not contravene the Constitution or federal laws.[39] Such orders and Decrees represent an important source of LL. They cover different areas of LL (such as wages of employees at budget-financed organizations, status of public servants and so on).[40]

§5. Legal Acts of the Government and Other Executive Bodies

176. Other important sources of Russian LL are decisions, orders and other legal acts issued by the Government of the RF. These acts may be adopted on the basis of and pursuant to the Constitution, federal laws and normative Decrees of the President. Should the acts of the Government contravene the Constitution, federal laws and the Decrees of the President, they may be repealed by the President.[41]

177. A further source of LL in the RF is normative documents issued by Ministries and other state bodies of executive power. In this respect the MLSP of the RF should be mentioned.

178. A number of other federal executive bodies are also empowered to issue normative acts within the powers given to them by federal legislation, Decrees of the President or Orders (Decisions) of the Government. For example, appropriate executive state bodies (such as ministries, departments, state committees or state services) of the RF issue orders and instructions that normally cover workers of the industries concerned, or groups of industries.

39. Article 90 of the RF Constitution.
40. *See also* paras 12, 182 and 189.
41. Article 115 of the RF Constitution.

§6. Legal Acts of Subjects of the RF

179. Since labour legislation falls under the joint jurisdiction of the RF and the subjects of Federation, legal acts adopted by the subjects of the RF seem to be an important source too. The RF LC provides the list of matters falling within the exclusive federal jurisdiction. At the same time, Article 6 of the RF LC empowers the subjects of the RF to create labour legislation on any other matter that goes beyond this exclusive jurisdiction. In this case, a higher level of workers' rights and social guarantees (as compared with established by federal legislation) resulting in an increase of budget expenses or in a decrease of budget revenues has to be ensured at the expense of the budget of a respective subject.

The subjects of the RF can also legislate on matters that have not been regulated at the federal level. Upon the adoption of the federal level legislation on the same matters, the respective legislation of the subject of the RF has to be brought into compliance with the federal legislation. Should the legislation of the subject contradict the LC (or any other federal legislation), or diminish the level of employee rights and social guarantees ensured at the federal level, the provisions of the LC or other federal legislation are applied in the respective subject of the RF.

In practice legislation adopted by subjects of the Federation often covers important spheres of LL. For example, a number of normative legal acts were adopted by Moscow City Duma (e.g., the Law of Moscow 'On Social Partnership' of 22 October 1997 No. 44 (with following amendments); and the Law of Moscow 'On Registration of Foreign Labour in Moscow' of 19 September 2001 No. 51). In developing these laws, subordinate normative acts were adopted by the Moscow Government (such as Resolution of 25 January 2000 No. 53 'On the Procedure for Arranging of Public Works in Moscow'; and Resolution of 28 December 1999 No. 1228 'On Obligatory Preventive Medical Examinations and Hygienic Certification').[42]

§7. Legal Acts of Local Self-government

180. Labour regulations of local (municipal) self-governing bodies issued within their competencies are also considered as LL sources. These regulations must not contradict the LC and other federal legislation, as well as the acts adopted at the level of the subjects of the RF.[43] Such acts are applied in the territory of the appropriate administrative division.[44]

---

42. *See also* para. 189.
43. Article 5 of the RF LC.
44. *See also* para. 190.

§8. Collective Agreements

181. Collective agreements are recognized as legal acts. They may establish norms of working conditions, as well as social guarantees for employees in an occupation, sector of activity, specific territory, etc.

The term 'collective agreement' in its narrow sense means a legal act to regulate the social-labour relations between the employer and the employees of an enterprise or with an individual employer.[45] But collective agreements may also be at a range of levels (such as General Agreements and branch (inter-branch) agreements). They also may be bipartite or tripartite. *See also* paragraphs 519 and 523–526.

182. The highest level of tripartite collective agreements is represented by the General Agreement. One of the parties to it is the RF Government. This type of agreement was introduced by the Presidential Decree 'On Social Partnership and Disputes Settlement' of 15 November 1991 as a new instrument of labour policy. Current General Agreement was concluded for the period of years 2018–2020. *See also* paragraph 526.

§9. Work Rules and Other Local Sources

183. A specific feature of Russian LL is the existence of local sources of law (so-called local normative legal acts) which are not included into legislation. Local normative legal acts containing LL rules are applied within an appropriate organization (an employer).

184. The main condition for regulating labour relations at local level is participation of employees (their representatives).

For the purposes of adopting other local legal acts, the LC establishes the following forms of employees' participation:

(a) taking into account the opinion of the representative body of the employees (in cases envisaged in the LC, other laws and other normative legal acts, as well as collective agreement). For example, work rules at an enterprise may be adopted by an employer only in accordance with this procedure; and
(b) coordinating with the representative body of employees.

Under the established procedures, an employer enables to adopt such local acts as Work Rules of an Enterprise; Regulations on Wages and Bonuses; and Regulations on Working Time and Rest. The LC also makes reference to some local acts which are necessary to be issued by an employer.

Regarding concluding of collective agreements, such participation is realized through procedures of collective bargaining. *See* paragraphs 529 and 530.

---

45. Article 40 of the RF LC.

185. According to the general rule of validity of local normative acts, such acts weakening the position of the employees as compared to the labour legislation, collective agreement, as well as if they were adopted without observing the above procedure, are considered as invalid.

§10. Relationship (Hierarchical Order) Between the Different Sources

186. Labour legislation is applied in accordance with hierarchy of normative acts. This hierarchy primarily is followed from the RF Constitution.

187. The Constitution of the RF has supreme legal force and direct effect and is applicable throughout the entire territory of the RF.

Laws and other legal acts adopted by the RF may not contravene the Constitution.

Federal laws may not contravene federal constitutional laws.

188. The principles of hierarchy of federal laws are also followed from the RF LC. As the Article 5 of the RF LC prescribes, this Code has a higher position in labour legislation. It means that labour standards established by other legal acts (including other federal laws) must comply with the LC. In case of conflict of rules, the LC applies.

189. Another principle of hierarchy is explained by the federative structure of the RF. Labour legislation adopted by subjects of RF may not contradict federal legislation (the RF LC, other federal laws, Decrees of the President of the RF, decisions of the Government of the RF, other normative legal acts of the federal bodies of executive power).

According to the RF Constitution, labour legislation is the sphere of joint jurisdiction of the RF and its subjects. At the same time, the LC distributes the competence between the RF and its subjects. In particular Article 6 of the LC clearly defines that the following questions are regulated on federal level:

(a) main principles of state policy in the sphere of labour relations and other relations directly associated with them;
(b) fundamentals of LL;
(c) the level of labour rights, liberties and guarantees to employees (including additional guarantees to individual categories of employees) ensured by the state;
(d) procedure of concluding, changing and terminating of employment contracts;
(e) fundamentals of social partnership, procedure of arranging collective negotiations and concluding and changing of collective agreements;
(f) procedure for resolving of individual and collective labour disputes;
(g) principles and procedures of state monitoring and control over observation of labour legislation, including the system and procedure of controlling in the sphere of safety at work;
(h) procedure of investigation of industrial accidents and occupational diseases;

(i) system and procedure of carrying out of state expert evaluation of the working conditions and certification of industrial objects regarding their compliance with the safety requirements;
(j) conditions of material liability of employees and employers;
(k) types of disciplinary sanctions and procedure of their application;
(l) system of state statistical reporting pertaining to labour and safety issues; and
(m) particulars of legal regulation of the work of individual categories of employees.

Consequently, the subjects of the RF may create legislation on matters outside the above spheres of competence of the Federation. It should be noted, that the competence of federal bodies in the sphere of LL can be delegated to the subjects of the Federation (LC as amended by the RF Law of 3 July 2016).

190. Taking into account the existence of local sources of LL, it has to be mentioned that local legal normative acts, as well as legal acts of the bodies of local government containing the norms of labour legislation, may not contradict the RF LC, other federal laws, Decrees of the President of the RF, decisions (Orders) of the Government of the RF, other normative legal acts of the federal bodies of executive power, laws and other normative legal acts of the subjects of the RF.

191. It is necessary to stress that some legal acts adopted by the USSR are still in force. Until harmonization of legislation of the former Soviet Union, such acts are applicable insofar as they do not contravene to the LC.[46]

§11. International LL

192. International law is also considered as the source of Russian LL. The commonly recognized principles and norms of international law as well as international treaties signed by the RF constitute an integral part of its legal system. If an international treaty signed by the RF stipulates other rules than those stipulated by the LL of the RF, the rules of the international treaty apply. International norms also prevail if they set more favourable conditions for workers than the Russian legislation does.[47]

193. The ILO Conventions which are ratified by the RF also serve as sources of Russian LL.

The Soviet Union ratified fifty ILO Conventions. Of this forty-three retained their force in the RF as the legal successor of the USSR. By 1 January 2016 seventy-five ILO Conventions had the status of ratified Conventions in the RF.

Beginning from 1998 General Agreements, concluded between the RF Government, All Russian Trade Unions and Russian Union of Employers, are supplemented with a list of the ILO Conventions recommended by the parties concerned

46. Article 423 of the RF LC.
47. Article 15(4) of the RF Constitution.

for consideration and further ratification. The General Agreement for 2000–2001 recommended to consider ratification of Conventions 'On Compensation in Case of Occupational Diseases' (42), 'Minimum Standards of Social Security' (102), 'On Basic Aims and Standards of Social Policy' (117), 'Termination of Employment' (158), 'Protection of Workers' Claims in case of Employer's Bankruptcy' (173) and others. In 2010 Russia has ratified the ILO Convention (132) On Paid Leaves. During the period of time between 2010 and 2014, such Conventions as NN 187, 154, 185, 173, 176, 140 and some others were ratified.

Russia is regarded to be a country with a relatively high number of ratified ILO Conventions. Norms and rules determined by ILO documents are included in many Russian laws regulating labour relations even though the relevant ILO Conventions have not been ratified.

194. In February 1996 Russia joined the European Council and thus acquired a number of obligations, including one to ratify the 'Convention on Human Rights and Basic Liberties', which guarantees political rights to all citizens and empowers the European Court on Human Rights to supervise their implementation. The above convention was ratified by Russia in 1998.

The European Social Charter was signed by the RF, but it has not been ratified yet.

195. Russia is a member of the CIS under the resolution of the Supreme Council of the RSFSR No. 2014-I 'On Ratification of the Treaty of Establishment of the Commonwealth of Independent States' of 12 December 1991. Conventions and Treaties of the CIS sighed by the RF are also the sources of LL. For example, Russia signed an Agreement regarding labour migration and social protection of migrant workers (signed by twelve state members of the CIS in April 1994).

§12. Judge-made Law

196. According to the legal theory, the decisions of the courts are not officially regarded as sources of law. Nevertheless, it is recognized that they play a very important role in the practical realization of law, including LL. This is especially so for the decisions of higher courts that have the competence to resume and to interpret the practice of lower courts. Therefore it is mainly noticed that if court decisions are not applied in case of making resumes by judges, they are not recognized as sources of law, being very important and integral part of legal system and in some aspects defining the development of law practice.

197. It is necessary to take into account the Decisions of the RF Supreme Court in this monograph. In this respect the Decision of the Plenary Session of the Supreme Court of the RF of 17 March 2004 'On Application of the Labour Code of the Russian Federation by the Courts of the RF', with additions of December 2006, should be mentioned. For the purposes of defining of legal nature of employment relationships, recently adopted Decision of the Plenary Session of the Supreme Court of the RF of 29 May 2018 N15 should be referred to.

198. Constitutional reviews issued by the Constitutional Court of the RF are also not recognized as sources of law. At the same time, they assist the legislature to better understand whether or not to apply the legal rules with contradictions. When the Constitutional Court of the RF recognizes the act (the rule) to be unconstitutional, the appropriate act (the rule) shall not apply. Some decisions of this Court are also important to the LL. In particular, in May 1986 a standard was introduced in the LC of 1971 which permitted termination of employment caused by the retirement of the employee. This standard was declared to be unconstitutional by the RF Constitutional Court in February 1992.

In 15 March 2005 the Constitutional Court of the RF confirmed the right of owners of an enterprise to dismiss managers without any explanation of reasons. At the same time, it declared Article 279 of the RF LC to be unconstitutional in the part which does not provide for minimum severance pay in such cases. As a result, the appropriate changes have been included in the current LC (in 2006).

Chapter 6. International Private LL

199. The LC must be observed on the entire territory of the RF by all employers, as well as by all foreign individuals, companies and international organizations in Russia. See paragraph 112. This means, *inter alia*, that employees – the citizens of the RF – enjoy all the rights prescribed by LL. It does not depend on the status of an employer.

§1. The Employment of Foreign Citizens in the RF

200. The RF Law No. 11-FZ of 25 July 2002 'On Legal Status of Foreign Citizens in the RF', with following amendments, prescribes that foreign citizens have the rights in the sphere of realizing their abilities to work in the territory of the RF. Foreigners are not allowed to participate in public service in the RF.

At the same time, the legislation on employment establishes special permissive procedures in this respect. These procedures oblige an employer to obtain the appropriate permissive document for employment of foreign labour force in the RF.

Moreover an acknowledgement (a permissive document giving a foreign citizen the right to be employed in the RF) must also be received by the foreign citizen.

Since 2014 the RF LC has regulated the particulars of hiring of foreign employees in its separated Chapter 50.1.

201. The above permissive procedure is not applicable to some categories of foreign citizens, in particular the following citizens:

(a) officially recognized as refugees;
(b) permanently or temporarily living in the RF;
(c) employees of diplomatic and consular institutions as well as organizations having diplomatic status;
(d) scholars working in the institutions established in accordance with Russian intergovernmental (exchange) agreements;
(e) journalists accredited in the RF;
(f) students having practical training during their vacations in the framework of programs of Russian educational establishments for higher professional education; and
(g) persons for whom another employment procedure is stipulated by intergovernmental agreements between the RF and foreign countries as well as by normative legal acts of the RF, and some others.

202. The registration of foreign citizens or persons without citizenship as a foreign worker is evidenced by the registration licence. For instance, in Moscow this licence is issued for a period not exceeding one year. Regarding Moscow city, this procedure is described in more detail in the corresponding regulations, adopted by the Law of Moscow of 19 September 2001 No. 51 'On the Accounting of Foreign Labour Force in Moscow'. *See also* paragraphs 155–157.

§2. The Employment of Russian Citizens Abroad

203. The legislation regulating the employment of Russian citizens abroad is relatively complicated. The RF Law on Employment states that intermediary activity on promotion of employment abroad may be realized with participation of agencies (both state and private). In this respect private agencies shall have a special permit (licence) to realize the activity thereof. Such a licence is issued for a definite period of time and in accordance with the requirements defined by legislation (mainly by the Order issued by the RF Government).

204. Work abroad may be also realized in accordance with international agreements with participation of the RF. RF entered into international agreements signed by the countries – the members of CIS (e.g., The Agreement on Cooperation in the Sphere of Labour Migration, made in 15 April 1994 by twelve members of the CIS). Russia also concluded agreements with other countries (for instance, the Agreement 'On Employment of Workers Aimed to Improving of Their Professional and Language Knowledge', which was signed between the RF and Germany).[48]

205. Russian LL establishes particularities of regulating the labour of employees assigned to work in diplomatic missions and consular institutions of the RF and in foreign missions of Federal Executive Agencies and State Institutions of the RF.[49] A contract of employment with the workers above shall be made for a period of up to three years. At the end of the indicated period, a labour contract may be renewed for a new term. At the end of the service abroad, such a worker must be granted his previous or an equivalent job (office), or in the absence of such a position and with his consent, a different job (office).[50] The rules of international private LL should be also referred to in this respect.

Regarding termination of a contract of employment with Russian employees engaged in employment abroad, *see also* paragraph 387.

48. Kurennoy, A.M., *International Labour Law, in: Labour Law of Russia (Textbook)*, Moscow: Moscow State University, 'Jurist', 2004, p. 476.
49. Chapter 53 of the RF LC.
50. Article 338 of the RF LC.

Part I. The Individual Employment Relationship

Chapter 1. Definitions and Concepts

§1. Contract of Employment

206. The contract of employment is recognized as an agreement between the employer and the employee in accordance with which the employer must provide the job to the employee with the work function agreed upon, ensure the working conditions as stipulated by the LC and other normative legal acts, as well as collective agreements and local acts and pay wages to the employee timely and in full, while the employee undertakes to perform the work determined by the agreement personally, under the control and management of the employer and to comply with the internal working regulations in effect in the organization.[51]

207. By concluding an employment contract, an employee enters an employment relationship. The current LC provides the definition of an employment relationship.[52] It is based on the agreement between the employer and employee on the personal fulfilment of a labour function (work in a certain occupation, qualification, position or in accordance with a definite type of given work) for payment. As distinct from other relationships arising in the sphere of labour performance (such as those based on civil law contracts), an employment relationship primarily means an engagement in subordinate, dependent work. There are also additional criteria which help to determine the employment relationship (e.g., work undertaken is a broader group of tasks belonging to a 'type of job' as distinct from the definite work (task) product or services undertaken by independent contractor as a party for contracts concluded under civil law; an employee has automatically been included on the staff of workers (or personnel), whereas an employer has the right of organizing and managing the staff.[53]

208. The employment relationship is based on a contract of employment concluded in compliance with the LC. At the same time, in cases and according to the procedure specified by laws, other normative legal acts or internal documents of an

51. Article 56 of the RF LC.
52. Article 15 of the RF LC.
53. *See also* paras 69–71.

enterprise, employment relationships may arise as a result of election to a certain position; court decision; and admission to work on the order of the employer or his representative regardless of whether the labour contract has been drawn up appropriately. Mainly such situations include special categories of employee.

§2. The Different Categories of Employee

I. Leading Personnel

209. To define the legal status of leading personnel is very complicated. From the legal point of view, the status of leaders of enterprises is established by different branches of legislation, mainly by civil and LL, as well as by the foundation documents of an enterprise and by a contract of employment. The current LC contains a special chapter regulating employment relationships with leaders of enterprises and members of collective executive bodies of organizations. At the same time, the competence of such employees also follows from federal laws defining the status of the appropriate organizations. For example, the competence of a chief (usually called as a general director) of a joint-stock company is mostly derived from the RF Law 'On Joint-stock Companies'. According to this law, the operation of labour legislation of the RF extends to relations between the company and the one-person executive body of the company (e.g., general director) and/or members of the collegial executive body of the company (management board, directorate), in that part which is not contrary to the provisions of this federal law. It means that LC does not have priority in case of contradiction of these two legal acts.[54]

210. The owner (owners) of an enterprise may invite the organization, as well as an individual entrepreneur for the purposes of leading by its company entity. Neither of these situations is covered by LL.

The LC states that its provisions are applied to all organization heads notwithstanding their type and the type of their property excluding the following cases:

(1) the chief of an organization is its only participant (a founder), or a single member of organization, as well as the only owner of its property (e.g., Russian legislation prescribes that the member may exist only in the case of a limited liability company);[55]
(2) an organization is managed under a contract with another managing organization or an individual entrepreneur (manager).[56]

211. In case of concluding an employment contract with the leader of organization, first the LC applies. The Code provides a special status for such employees. In particular an employment contract with a leader of organization may be concluded

54. *See also* para. 116.
55. The RF Law No. 14-FZ of 8 Feb. 1998 'On Limited Liability Companies', with subsequent amendments and additions.
56. Article 273 of the RF LC.

only for a definite period of time depending on foundation documents or an agreement of the parties. This contract may be terminated earlier without established reasons. The leader of an organization has to bear full material liability for direct actual damages caused to an organization, which is different from other employees. Moreover in cases provided by federal law the leader must compensate for losses caused by his/her culpable actions in accordance with civil legislation[57] (in particular, this possibility may occur regarding leaders of joint-stock companies).

The above rules may also be applied to the members of collective executive bodies of enterprises.[58]

Some aspects of legal status of leading personnel are interpreted by courts practice of the RF Supreme Court. In this respect the Decision of Plenum of this court of 2 June 2015 N21 should be referred to.

212. Some limitations are also stated by special legislation. For example, in accordance with the RF Law of 14 November 2002 No. 161-FZ 'On State and Municipal Companies' (Article 21), the head of a state company must not occupy any other position or be engaged in any other paid business in state bodies, commercial or non-profit-making organizations, except education or any other creative activity.

II. Temporary Work

213. The situations of employment with participation of private agencies have received practical importance in recent years. Well-known as agency work, in Russia this type of employment is mainly called 'leasing of personnel' or 'rented work', and it has become more widespread. It occurs where a worker is engaged by an intermediary private employment agency. Most of these agencies provide the services which may be recognized as temporary agency work. For example, the service of using casual employees who perform certain work within time periods lasting from several hours to several months (or longer) by a company is recognized as one of the most required. These employees are included in the staff of the agency, but they work in a company that needs such personnel. Meanwhile this type of work is regulated by the RF LC (Chapter 53.1). In accordance with the Article 341.2 of the LC, the employment agency offers its experts (workers) for the following purposes:

(a) to replace staff personnel for the duration of their leave, illness, missions, studies by providing assistants, secretaries, finance clerks and bookkeepers;

57. Article 5 of the CC states that a person whose right has been violated may demand full compensation of the damages suffered, if the law or a contract does not provide for compensation of damages in lesser amounts.
58. Article 281 of the RF LC.

(b) to work in individual projects by sending analysts, administrative personnel, engineers and technicians, commercial representatives and other temporary work during the period of time not more than nine months;
(c) to perform seasonal work for promoters, merchandisers, etc.

Previously it was difficult to identify the precise legal status of the workers engaged. Current Russian labour legislation (as well as social security) has made references to such situations. The agencies employ workers under conditions of employment contracts and are required by law to provide workers with full written details of the terms and conditions of employment, including the type of work, the rates of pay (in additional agreement to the contract) and so on. It is necessary to stress that under Russian legislation, an agency worker is entitled to the same basic employment conditions as would have received if recruited for the job directly by client (e.g., an enterprise). Basic employment conditions are those included in contracts, as well as existed in local normative acts and collective agreements (if any). They include right to equal pay, as well as compensations for hazard works.

214. It should be noted that RF LC makes reference to so-called temporary contracts, which are recognized as specific contracts of employment. Traditionally they do not cover the above-mentioned temporary agency work. Temporary contracts are concluded for a very short time (that is why they are recognized as a specific type of fixed-term contract). The LC provides the same level of state guarantees for employees involved in such temporary contracts (e.g., paid leave).[59] Their status has other specific features regarding grounds for termination of employment, as well as procedure and notification.[60]

III. Seasonal Workers

215. Seasonal jobs are recognized to be those that by virtue of climatic or other natural conditions are performed during a certain period (season), not exceeding six months.[61] The legal status of employees involved is also characterized by some specifics as concern termination of employment (*see* paragraph 395).

IV. Transport Workers

216. The RF LC contains a separate chapter on particulars of the legal status of transport workers. Workers hired for jobs directly associated with vehicular traffic must go through a professional selection and training process under procedures established by a federal executive body for the relevant type of transportation.[62] The

59. Article 291 of the RF LC.
60. *See* para. 402.
61. Article 293 of the RF LC.
62. Article 328 of the RF LC.

hiring of a worker for a job directly associated with vehicular traffic is completed only after an obligatory preliminary medical examination.

Transport workers are regulated to a greater extent by additional sub-legislation, which especially concerns their working time.

217. Russian LL provides more strict disciplinary sanctions for transport employees. In this respect the Code of Internal Water Transport (of 2000, with amendments), as well as the statute of On Discipline of Workers of Fishing (approved by the Decision of the Government of the RF No. 708 of 21 September 2000, applied with subsequent amendments) may be mentioned.

Among established disciplinary sanctions for railway transport workers, the temporary prohibition on performing job functions (which is not prescribed by the RF LC) should be referred to.[63]

V. Employees Working and Living in the Regions of the Far North and Comparable Areas

218. The legal status of the above category of employees is defined by the RF LC. The RF Law 'On State Guarantees and Compensations to Persons Working and Living in the Regions of the Far North and the Districts Being Equal Thereto'[64] is also applied. The Russian state establishes additional guarantees for these employees. Currently such guarantees and allowances are set by the federal laws in the organizations backed by the Federal Budget; by the laws of the subjects of the RF in the organizations backed by the budgets of the subjects; and set in the organizations backed by the local budgets by the municipal legal acts, while in the organizations which are not backed by the public budgets, they are set by the employer. The guarantees include an additional coefficient for wages, additional days off and some other features.

VI. Teaching Personnel

219. It should be noted that there are differences in the status of teaching personnel depending on the levels of schools or institutions where they work. Scientific and teaching positions in institutions (e.g., universities) of higher education may be occupied under a fixed-term contract, as well as under a contract for an indefinite period of time.[65] The positions of dean of a college (university) and of a faculty (e.g., law faculty), as well as of the head of a department (e.g., the Department of Labour Law) in institutions of higher education are elected. Procedures for elections to the indicated positions are defined by the charters of institutions of

63. The Regulations on Discipline of Workers of Railway Transport, approved by the Decision of the RF Government No. 621 of 25 Aug. 1992.
64. The RF Law No. 4520-1 of 19 Feb. 1993 'On State Guarantees and Compensations to Persons Working and Living in the Regions of the Far North and the Districts Being Equal Thereto' (with subsequent additions and amendments, most recently in 2018).
65. Article 332 of the RF LC.

higher education. For contracts with other teaching personnel of higher institutions, a competitive selection procedure is in place.

220. Legislation on education establishes some restrictions in the sphere of employing teachers. Persons who are prohibited from such activity by a court sentence or medical indication, and also those convicted of certain crimes, are not allowed to engage in teaching activity. There are also some other particulars in legal regulations of work of teaching personnel (e.g., reduced working time and special rules on providing leaves).

VII. Apprentices

221. The RF LC prescribes two types of apprenticeship contracts:

(1) a contract for professional training with a person seeking work; and
(2) a contract for retraining without a separation from work with an employee of the given organization.

Previously an apprenticeship contract for professional training with a person seeking work was recognized as a civil law contract; the current RF LC does not contain such a provision. An apprenticeship contract with an employee of a given organization is a supplemental one to the contract of employment. This type of apprenticeship contract is governed by labour legislation.[66] The RF LC makes reference to such a contract, as well as its validity and termination. Employees undergoing training in an organization may, by agreement with the employer, be fully released from their work pursuant to the contract or may perform the work on terms of a part-time work.[67] If a trainee fails to perform his obligations under the contract without valid reasons upon the conclusion of an apprenticeship, he or she shall, at the employer's request, refund a stipend received during the apprenticeship, as well as reimbursing other expenses sustained by the employer in connection with the apprenticeship.[68]

VIII. Workers Employed by Individual Employers

222. The Russian LC, as well as legal acts of the RF Government, stresses that workers employed by individual employers should enjoy the same scope of the rights provided by labour legislation. In particular an individual employer is required to draw up an employment contract with the worker in writing, to register that contract with the corresponding local government body. He/she is also obliged to pay the most of insurance contributions and other mandatory payments for the

66. Article 198 of the RF LC.
67. Article 203 of the RF LC.
68. Article 207 of the RF LC.

purposes of social insurance of workers engaged. Upon agreement of the parties, the contract between an employee and an individual employer may be made for either a definite or indefinite time.[69]

At the same time, there is a specific procedure for termination of the contract.[70]

IX. Homeworkers

223. The RF LC contains a separate chapter regulating the status of homeworkers. According to the definition provided by the LC, a homeworker is considered to be a person who enters an employment contract to perform work at home, using materials, tools and machines issued by the employer or acquired by the workers at their own expense. If a homeworker uses his/her own tools and machines, he or she must be compensated for it.[71] *See also* paragraph 385.

In a connection with homeworkers, such a new type of employees as distanced workers (or teleworkers) should be mentioned. This type of work is defined as labour activity out of the location of an employer and is realized directly or indirectly under control of the employer, under conditions of using to its accomplishment information and public telecommunication networks, including the Internet network. The conclusion of employment contracts with such employees is made by exchanging of documents through Internet and signed in electronic form. All necessary aspects of employment are defined by individual employment contract (Chapter 49.1 of the LC).

X. Shift Work

224. Work in shifts is a special way of executing work functions out of the place of residence of the employees when they cannot return to their place of residence on a daily basis. Work in shifts is applied when the place of work is far away from the office of employer with the purpose of reducing the period of construction, repair and reconstruction of industrial, social and other objects in thinly populated, far regions or regions with unfavourable environment.[72]

A shift is understood to be a total period including time of work and time of breaks between shifts. Shift time is not allowed to exceed one month. In exceptional cases the employer may increase shift time up to three months on certain objects taking into account the opinion of an elected trade union of this organization.[73]

69. Chapter 48 of the RF LC.
70. *See also* paras 114 and 392.
71. Article 310 of the RF LC.
72. Article 297 of the RF LC.
73. Article 299 of the RF LC.

225. Guarantees and compensation payments to shift workers are provided by legislation. The current LC states that employees involved in shift work by organizations backed by the Federal Budget are paid an allowance, the procedure and the amount determined by the Government of the RF. To the employees of the organizations backed by the budgets of the subjects of the RF and local budgets, allowance for the shift work is paid according to the procedure set at the level of the subject or the local authority, respectively. To employees of organizations which are not backed by public budgets, allowance for shift work is paid according to the procedure set by the employer (by a collective agreement, other local acts adopted with the participation of employees) or by a contract of employment.[74]

XI. Blue-collar and White-collar Workers

226. In general the current LL does not distinguish between the above categories of workers. The exclusion may be found regarding employees involved in relationships with organizations financed by state budgets.[75]

§3. Different Categories of Employment Contract

227. Russian LL prescribes that employment contracts may be concluded for the following period:

(1) an indefinite period of time; and
(2) a definite period of time (fixed-term contracts) – for a specified period of not more than five years or for a period of the fulfilment of specified work.

I. Fixed-term Contracts

228. There is a general rule that fixed-term contracts may be used when employment relations cannot be established for an indefinite period taking into account the character of the forthcoming work, or the conditions of its fulfilling or the interests of worker. While previous labour legislation generally limited use of fixed-term contract arrangements by the nature of the work, the current LC (Article 59) specifically extends the possibilities of fixed-term employment arrangements regarding the following categories of employees, as well as the situations listed below:

(a) heads of companies, their deputies and chief accountants;
(b) on the agreement of parties – with employees in small business enterprises (up to thirty-five employees), in trade companies (up to 20) and those employed by individual entrepreneurs;
(c) employees working outside Russia;

74. Article 302 of the RF LC.
75. *See also* paras 330 and 340.

(d) retired persons (on the agreement of parties);
(e) to replace a temporarily absent employee preserving his job according to the law;
(f) for the period of fulfilling temporary works (up to two months), as well as seasonal works or agency works (*see* paragraph 213);
(g) persons hired for work in the organizations located in the regions of the Far North and comparable territories;
(h) to carry out urgent works to prevent incidents, accidents, disasters, epidemics, epizootic diseases, as well as to eliminate the consequences of these and other emergencies;
(i) to carry out works outside the usual range of activities of the organization (reconstruction, installation, start-up and testing and other works), as well as to carry out works pertaining to the expansion of production capacities or the volume of rendered services known to be of temporary nature (up to one year);
(j) persons hired for work in the organizations known to be created for a certain period of time or known to fulfil a certain job;
(k) persons hired to carry out certain known work in cases when the particular date of its fulfilment (termination) cannot be defined;
(l) persons undergoing day-time studies;
(m) persons, according to the health condition certified by the medical statement, permitted to work part-time only;
(n) on agreement with creative personnel of mass media, organizations of cinematography, theatres, theatrical and concert organizations, circuses, as well as professional sportsmen according to the list of professions endorsed by the Government of the RF with participation of the RTC;
(o) scientific, pedagogical and other workers having concluded labour contracts for a definite period of time as a result of the contest arranged according to the procedure specified by the law or other normative legal act of the body of state power or body of local government;
(p) in case of election for a definite period of time to an elective body or elective position for a paid job, as well as being hired for work pertaining directly to activities of the members of elective bodies or officials in the bodies of state power and bodies of local government, as well as in political parties and other public associations;
(q) persons (mostly registered unemployed) sent for temporary works by state employment service, including public works and some others.

Other cases for concluding fixed-term contracts may be envisaged in the federal laws. As follows from the above, in some cases fixed-term contracts may be concluded only on agreement between an employer and employee.

If a fixed-term employment contract is concluded, it should indicate its effective time period and the circumstances (reasons) that served as the basis for its conclusion.

II. Contracts for an Indefinite Period of Time

229. In spite of their great range, fixed-term contracts are regarded as exceptional and to be concluded in cases strictly stipulated by legislation. Russian LL implies as a general rule, the use of contracts of employment for an indefinite period.

It should be noted that if a fixed-term employment contract does not specify its effective time period, the contract is considered to be concluded for an indefinite period of time. If none of the parties demand discontinuation of the fixed-term contract upon its expiry, and the employee continues his/her work after the expiry of the effective time period of the contract, it is also considered to be concluded for indefinite time period. A fixed-term employment contract concluded without the above-mentioned grounds, as established by the State Labour Inspection or by a court, is considered to be concluded for indefinite period of time.

§4. The Conclusion and the Form of the Contract

I. Form of the Contract

230. Under Russian LL a contract of employment must be concluded in writing. The RF LC requires that an employer issues the Order regarding hiring of the employee. This Order is issued upon conclusion of an employment contract. The Order has to be declared to the employee in three days beginning from the day of conclusion of the contract with him/her. It is necessary to stress that the fact of establishing of an employment relationship follows from the fact of conclusion of the contract of employment.

In some cases electronic signature is accepted (for instance, concerning distanced employees). *See* paragraph 223.

231. An employer must inform employees about the internal work rules of the enterprise, other local normative acts that are relevant to the job activity of the employee, as well as about the terms of a collective agreement applied.

II. Documents Required

232. The LC contains the list of documents that an employer may request from an applicant at the time of hiring.[76] In particular these are as follows:

(a) passport (or other personal identification document);
(b) workbook (a document which proves previous professional experience if any, *see* paragraph 233), except when a contract of employment is concluded for the first time, or when an employee starts working at a secondary job (is involved in secondary employment or undertaking multiple jobs);

76. Article 65 of the RF LC.

(c) insurance certificate issued for the purposes of obligatory pension insurance;
(d) military record documents – for employees who are subjects to call-up; and
(e) diploma or other certificate of education, qualification or special training – for jobs that require special knowledge or special training.

In some cases additional documents may also be required by employer. It is forbidden to require additional documents from employee, except documents that are mentioned in the RF LC, as well as by other legislation.

III. Workbooks

233. An employer is responsible for issuing a workbook as concerns an employee who is concluding a contract of employment for the first time. A workbook reflects all the professional activity of an employee (except disciplinary sanctions applied). An employer (except individual employers – physical persons) must keep workbooks for all employees who have worked in an organization for more than five days, presuming that this organization is the primary job place of these employees. Information about a secondary job place can be recorded in a service record book at primary job place on request of employee, presuming that the employee provides correspondent documents proving that employee is indeed working at a secondary job place. The RF LC, as well as the Decision of the RF Government No. 225 of 16 April 2003 'On Work Books', with subsequent amendments, regulates the main aspects regarding their completion and storage.

IV. Minimum Age

234. Both parties to a contract of employment must have a capacity to conclude this contract. The LC contains the rules governing the ability to conclude individual labour contracts.

235. The full capacity to a contract of employment is reached at the age of 16. If they have left main secondary education or a secondary educational institution in compliance with the federal law, the contract may be concluded by persons having reached 15 years of age.

At the same time, there is some limitation on employers concluding the contracts with minors between 15 (14) and 18 years of age. With consent of one of the parents (trustee) and the body of trusteeship, an employment contract may be concluded with a student having reached 14 years of age to carry out easy work not producing any harm to his health and not interfering in the process of study in the time free from study.[77]

236. In some spheres (such as theatres, cinematography, theatrical and concert organizations and circuses) it is even allowed to sign a contract of employment with

77. Article 63 of the RF LC.

persons under 14. It should be noted that there are statutory restrictions on employing such children. For example, it is only permitted with the consent of one of the parents (trustee) and the body of trusteeship, and the involvement in such activity should not produce any damage to health and moral development.[78]

V. Probation

237. Probation may be stipulated by an agreement of the parties for the purpose of verifying the suitability of the employee with the work entrusted to him or her. The RF LC excludes some categories of employees from the possibility to establish a probation period for them (such as pregnant women, persons less than 18 years of age, persons elected for their position and some others).

A probationary period condition must be included in a contract of employment. If no probationary period condition is stated in the contract, then this means that an employee is accepted without a probationary period. During the probation, all provisions of LL regulations and respective collective agreements apply to the employee concerned.[79] For instance, the worker is empowered to terminate probation at his/her initiative at any time with a three-day written notice (Article 71 of the LC).

238. The RF LC restated the traditional provision that the maximum probation period cannot exceed three months. However, an extended six-month term is now introduced for certain categories of employees (including heads of companies, chief accountants and their deputies, as well as heads of branch and representative offices). The probation period does not include some periods of the worker's absence (e.g., because of temporary incapacity to work).

239. Both the employer and the employee have the obligation to notify each other in writing three days prior to the termination of the contract during the probation period. If the results of probation prove to be unsatisfactory, the employer may terminate the contract of employment before the probation period has expired. While terminating the contract within the probation period, the employer must inform the employee in writing about the reasons for termination. In this case the contract of employment is terminated without consultation with the appropriate trade union body, as well as without payment of severance pay. The worker concerned may appeal against the decision of the employer in the court of law.

If the employer makes no decision on the termination of the contract before the end of the probation period, the worker concerned is considered as having passed the probation and his/her employment relationship can be subject to termination on the usual terms applicable to contracts of employment.

78. Article 63 of the RF LC.
79. Article 70 of the RF LC.

VI. Medical Examinations

240. Regarding some categories of employees, obligatory preliminary medical examinations are established. The list of appropriate work is established by the legislation (mainly on the level of Decisions of the RF Government), for instance medical examinations are applied in such spheres as education, health care and medical organizations and so on.[80]

VII. The Concept of Factual Employment Relationship

241. The concept of so-called factual employment relationships is also used in Russian LL. It is explained by the RF LC as an exceptional situation. Normally a contract of employment comes into effect on the day of its signing by the employee and the employer, unless otherwise is set by federal law, as well as by the contract.

Another possibility occurs when an employment contract comes into the force on the day when the employee is actually admitted to work in accordance with the order of the employer (or the representative).[81] Such situation is recognized as a conclusion of the contract de facto.

One more possibility of establishing of employment relationships may occur in cases, when civil law contracts for works or services are recognized as employment ones, in accordance with legislation.

VIII. The Contents of the Contract

242. As compared to the previous legislation, the LC envisaged a broader range of mandatory provisions that need to be included into an employment contract.[82] These are as follows:

(1) place of work (stating the structural division);
(2) job commencement date (and the duration of a contract, if a fixed-term contract has been concluded);
(3) name of the position, profession, the qualification according to the organization's personnel arrangements or the specific work function– often it is defined in specific legal acts;
(4) the employee's rights and duties;
(5) the employer's rights and duties;
(6) description of the working conditions, compensations and benefits to the employees for hard, harmful and/or hazardous jobs;
(7) the work and rest and leisure routine (if it differs for the employee from the general rules in effect in the organization);

80. *See also* para. 425.
81. Article 61 of the RF LC.
82. Article 57 of the RF LC.

(8) wage or salary terms (including the basic wage rate or official salary of the employee, additional payments, allowances and incentives); and
(9) types of the social insurance and its terms directly linked to work activities.

243. An employment contract may envisage the terms of non-disclosure of secrets protected by the law (state or commercial secrecy), as well as other terms not impairing an employee's position as compared to legislation and collective agreements (for instance, as regards additional non-obligatory pension insurance).

§5. Restrictions on the Right of Contracting

244. Russian LL contains certain limitations in the sphere of concluding an employment contract. The scope and limitations as concern the freedom of a contract of employment in Russia follow from national legislation, as well as from international LL. In particular the RF has ratified the ILO Conventions on Forced Labour (No. 29, 1930) and on the Abolishing of Forced Labour (No. 105, 1957).

First, LL forbids any restrictions whatsoever on these grounds, or the giving of preferential treatment to job applicants, on the basis of gender, race, nationality, language, social origins, wealth, place of residence, attitude to religion, beliefs, membership of a non-governmental organization or any other circumstance not related to the professional qualifications of the employee.[83]

245. In accordance with international rules, the RF LC prohibits forced labour. In particular, the following situations are especially banned:

(a) work to maintain labour discipline; and
(b) work as punishment in case of participation in a strike and so on.

246. Under the RF LC, the term 'forced labour' also includes the following situations:

(a) disregard of set dates for payment of wages as well as their incomplete payment;
(b) the employer requiring the employee to perform his/her work duties when the employee is not provided with group or individual protection means or the work is hazardous to the employee's life or health.[84]

247. For the purpose of the LC forced labour does not include:

(a) work required by legislation on military duty and military service or the alternative civil service instead of the military service;

83. *See also* paras 433–434.
84. Article 4 of the RF LC.

(b) work performed in conditions of an emergency situation, in other words, in cases of the declared state of emergency or martial law, of a disaster or a threat of disaster (fires, floods, hunger, earthquakes, intense epidemics or epizootics) as well as in other situations threatening life or the normal living conditions of the whole population or its part; and
(c) work performed pursuant to the final court verdict under supervision of the official state bodies responsible for enforcing laws on serving sentences.

248. An employer is free in choosing with whom to conclude a contract. In this respect it is necessary to stress some exclusions. For example, an employer has to follow to the direct recommendation of the state employment service to hire some categories of persons (e.g., the disabled). *See* paragraphs 428–431.

249. It was for the first time in Russian LL when the current LC established requirements in the sphere of data protection. Mainly they follow from international rules existed in this sphere. An employer must follow some principles of privacy while asking questions connected to the private life of an applicant.[85]

250. Under the general rule conditions of a contract of employment worsening the position of employees in comparison with labour legislation, collective agreements and local legal sources are invalid. The administration of the enterprise together with employees' representatives only have the right to establish at their own expense additional labour and social privileges for all employees or some categories of employees as compared to the above listed acts. In particular, it is prohibited to determine by mutual consent of the parties to a contract of employment such terms as its ways of termination (except when it is prescribed by legislation), disciplinary sanctions, as well as means of material responsibility.

251. Some limitations of freedom of a contract are established by rules of changing of conditions of contacts of employment. The terms of an employment contract may be changed only in accordance with an agreement between the parties and in written form. Otherwise a number of additional requirements (such as limited period of changing) should be observed. For instance, changes of the essential working conditions, systems and amount of remuneration of labour, privileges, operating conditions, setting up and abolition of part-time, combining of jobs, change of categories and denomination of posts and others must be announced to an employee at least two months before.

§6. Invalidity of a Contract of Employment

252. A contract of employment is cancelled if the employee fails to start his/her work without any valid reasons from the day defined by the contract (or the next day after its coming into force).[86]

---

85. *See* paras 279–281.
86. Article 61 of the RF LC.

253. There is a general rule in accordance with which employment contracts cannot contain terms and conditions reducing the level of rights and guarantees to employees set by the LLs. Should such terms be included in contracts, they (terms) are not to be applied.[87]

The procedure for recognizing an employment contract to be void follows from civil law. Often it is suggested to apply in such cases the civil law rules regulating the recognition of contracts as invalid. According to Article 166 of RF CC, a transaction is invalid on the grounds established by this Code, or by virtue of being deemed as such by a court (contested transaction), or irrespective of such deeming (null transaction). An invalid transaction does not entail legal consequences, except for those which are connected with its invalidity, and it is invalid from the moment of its conclusion.

87. *See also* para. 541.

Chapter 2. Rights and Duties of the Parties to Employment

254. The theory of Russian LL includes rights and duties of the parties to employment in the content of the employment relationship. Rights and duties of an employee and an employer are also recognized as an essential element of an employment contract to be agreed upon.

The main rights and duties of the parties to a contract of employment follow from the RF Constitution (Article 37), the LC (mainly Articles. 21 and 22), other legislation, as well as from local normative acts at an enterprise and collective agreements.

§1. Duties of an Employee

I. The Duty to Carry Out the Work

255. One of the most important contractual obligations of an employee is the duty to work. First, an employee is obliged to perform in good faith his/her labour duties prescribed by the employment contract. The duties are also determined by general description of the type of work (e.g., lawyer and manager). In this respect the work to be performed by an employee is explained through such characteristics as profession and qualification. These concepts help to define the scope of the work to be realized by an employee. Regarding employees involved in organizations financed by state budget, they are defined by the Government.

The duties of an employee may also follow from the internal documents of an enterprise (organization). This mostly concerns leading personnel (for instance, leaders of departments, vice-chiefs, etc.).

The RF LC prohibits an employer from requiring fulfilment of the work which is not envisaged in the contract of employment.

II. The Duty to Obey Lawful and Reasonable Orders

256. Under the RF LC, internal labour order shall be determined by local normative acts of an employer, usually with participation of representatives of employees of a particular enterprise (organization). In practice internal labour order may be stated by different local sources – such as a collective agreement, working time regulation, acts of administration and so on. It should be noted that an employer may choose one or more legal forms to regulate labour internal order.

257. The employee's duty to obey rules of an internal labour order is detailed as one of the disciplinary duties. The latter are listed in the RF LC, as far as they may be prescribed by legislation. In particular, employees are obliged to work honestly and bona fide, observe the labour discipline and timely and precisely implement of administrative directions; increase the labour efficiency; improve quality of production; as well as observe technological discipline, requirements on safety conditions and industrial sanitary; and take care of property of the enterprise. Employees also have to observe instructions on labour protection. Such instructions shall be drawn up and approved by the administration of an enterprise. Employees are also obliged to observe the established requirements for handling of machines and devices and handling of issued facilities of individual protection.

If an employee does not realize the above obligation an employer may apply disciplinary sanctions. The list of such sanctions follows from labour legislation (including the RF LC) and may not be increased by local normative acts, or by an agreement between an employer and employee.

III. The Duty to Treat Carefully the Property of an Employer and of Other Employees

258. In order to guarantee the realization of this duty, Russian LL has established material responsibility for employees. In general this means an obligation of a party to an employment contract to compensate for damage caused. On the other hand, an employer is required to provide employees with the conditions necessary for due work and guarantee of complete safety of entrusted property.

259. As regards an employee, the framework of material liability may not become wider than is established by legislation. An employee is obliged to compensate the employer for direct actual damages caused to the employer. In this respect actual damages are understood as a real reduction of the employer's property or worsening of the condition of such property (including the property of third parties if the employer is responsible for safeguarding it), and also the necessity for an employer to make expenditures or excess payments for the acquisition or restoration of the property. An employee must also bear material liability both for direct actual damage caused by him to the employer, as well as for the damage which arose with the employer as a result of compensation of damage by the employer to other persons (third persons).

260. It should be noted that the amount of money to be compensated by an employee is limited. Material responsibility, as a rule, is limited by certain part of employee's wage and must not exceed the whole expense of caused damage except in cases stipulated by legislation. At the same time, it is possible to increase the material liability as compared to the employee's wage. Such situations are called 'full material responsibility'. They are strictly limited and directly follow from the legislation (mostly from the RF LC). For example, an employee's full material liability may occur in case of intentional causing of damages; and causing of damage as a result of a crime or an administrative offence, if this has been established by court or other respective state body.

261. Full responsibility in case of damages is usually applied in connection with civil law contract violations. This principle is stated by Article 15 of the RF CC and is called as 'compensation of losses'. In particular the person whose right has been violated can demand that all the losses inflicted on her/him be compensated for, unless the law or contract stipulates a smaller recovery. The losses imply the expenses that the person whose right had been violated incurred or will have to incur in order to restore the violated right, the loss or damage of his/her property (actual damage), as well as lost revenues he/she could have received (lost profit). If the right-breaker made gains in consequence of this, the victim has the right to demand that, besides other losses, the lost profit be recovered in the amount no less than such gains. The duty to compensate full losses also follows from Article 393 of the CC: a debtor (who may be a worker as a party to a civil law contract of performance of work or providing of services) shall be obliged to compensate the creditor for losses caused by the failure to perform or improper performance of an obligation. As concerns the rules, which are mostly relevant to the civil law contracts, the contractor shall be held liable for failure to keep safe the customer's materials, equipment or other property which came into the contractor's possession in connection with execution of the contract agreement (Article 714 of the RF CC). Obviously civil law liability is wider than material liability of employees.

It is necessary to add that some categories of employees may be obliged to compensate damages in accordance with principles established by civil legislation. This mostly concerns managers of enterprises (or other categories of leading personnel). It follows from the LC RF that material liability in full for damages caused to an employer may be established by an employment contract made with the head of an organization, deputy head or chief accountant.

IV. The Duty to Notify

262. There are two main cases in which an employee is obliged to notify an employer. One appears in case of termination of a contract of employment at the initiative of an employee.[88]

Another is connected with situations representing a threat to human life and health, preservation of property of the employer, when an employee is obliged to notify immediately his/her employer or its representative (mostly – someone of leading personnel who is responsible for hiring employees).

§2. Duties of an Employer

I. The Duty to Provide Work

263. An employer has the duty to provide an employee with the work stipulated by the employment contract and other appropriate legal acts. The requirements of the work may follow not only from an employment contract, but also from other documents (e.g., local normative acts).[89] An employer is obliged to provide the employees with equipment, tools, technical documentation and other means necessary for their execution of labour duties. This is one of the essential characteristics

88. *See* paras 377–379.
89. *See also* para 262.

of an employment contract (as compared to the contracts of performing of works and providing of services that are regulated by civil law).

II. The Duty to Provide Healthy Work Conditions

264. An employer is obliged to organize a workplace for an employee which corresponds to state standards of labour organization and health and according to the rules of an enterprise, including the collective agreement. This duty also means an obligation to provide full reliable information concerning the conditions of work and safety.

First, the Constitution of the RF obliges all employers to provide health and safety conditions at work. In particular it says in its Article 37 that everyone shall have the right to work under conditions meeting the requirements of safety and hygiene.

Second, the RF LC explains this duty in more detail in the chapter regulating protection of labour. In particular an employer is obliged to ensure:

(a) application of means of individual and collective defence of employees;
(b) training in safe methods and techniques of the fulfilment of work with regard to the protection of labour;
(c) monitoring of labour conditions at workplaces, as well as of the propriety of the use by employees of means of individual and collective protection;
(d) organizing of mandatory, preliminary (during the start of work) and periodic (during labour activity) medical examinations (tests) of employees in cases stipulated by the LC, laws and other regulations, and non-admittance of employees to the performance of labour duties by them without having undergone mandatory medical examinations (tests), as well as in the event of medical contraindications;
(e) prevention of emergency situations and preservation of employees' life and health during the occurrence of such situations, including the provision of first aid to victims; and
(f) investigation of accidents at work and occupational deceases.

265. The duty to provide healthy conditions of work may be seen in a connection with the duty to provide an employee to realize the right to have a rest, in particular to establish normal duration of working time, including reduced working time for some categories of employees, to provide weekly days off, as well as paid annual leaves. According to the RF Constitution, everyone has the right to rest and leisure (Article 37 of the RF Constitution).

III. The Duty to Pay Remuneration

266. This duty means that an employer is required to provide timely payment in full of earnings according to the qualification, complexity of labour, quantity and quality of the fulfilled work. Article 37 of the Constitution obliges all employers to pay the remuneration for work without any discrimination whatsoever and not below the statutory minimum wage.[90]

267. The RF LC provides definite responsibility of an employer in respect of paying remuneration. For example, an employer has the duty to compensate an employee for earnings not received in all instances of the illegal deprivation of his/her possibility to work. In particular, this obligation applies if wages were not received due to:

- illegal removal of an employee from work, dismissal thereof or transfer to other work; and
- delay by the employer to issue some documents (e.g., the workbook) connected to work, etc.

Material liability of an employer for delay in payments is also prescribed. In particular, in the event of a violation by an employer of the established period for payments (such as wages, payments in case of leave or dismissals and so on), the employer shall be required to pay them with the payment of interest (for every day of the delay).

IV. The Duty to Compensate Damages Caused to the Property of an Employee

268. An employer who has caused damage to the property of an employee shall compensate this damage in full. The amount of damage shall be calculated according to market prices in effect in the given locality at the time the damage was incurred.

V. The Duties Connected to Participation of Employees in Regulating the Labour Process

269. An employer has some duties in the sphere above, such as the duty to provide full and reliable information to representatives of employees which is necessary to conclude appropriate collective agreements and to control the fulfilment thereof. An employer is also obliged to hold collective negotiations, according to the procedure specified in the RF LC.

VI. The Duty to Provide Obligatory Social Insurance for Employees

270. An employee (in contrast with some other workers, for instance, parties to contracts concluded under civil law) should receive the widest scope of rights in the

90. *See* paras 330–332.

sphere of social insurance. The status of employee also defines the entitlement of the person to the majority of state social insurance schemes.

As was mentioned above, obligatory social insurance is financed by special social funds. An employer's obligation in this respect is limited to deducting social taxes, as well as social security contributions at source from the wages of employees. The appropriate rates are stated by legislation on taxation and by the Federal Law regulating obligatory social insurance, respectively.[91]

271. Regarding industrial accidents and occupational diseases, an employer is also obliged to investigate cases in accordance with established procedures.

VII. Duties in the Sphere of Personal Data Protection

272. The RF LC introduced new requirements for storage, receipt, use and protection of employees' personal data. These rules are based on the RF Constitution, as well as on international legal norms. Article 23 of the Constitution proclaims that everyone shall have the right to privacy, to personal and family secrets, and to protection of their honour and good name. Everyone shall have the right to privacy of correspondence, telephone communications, mail and other communications. Any restriction of this right shall be allowed only under an order of a court of law.

Article 24 of the RF Constitution also states that it shall be forbidden to gather, store, use and disseminate information on the private life of any person without his/her consent. The bodies of state authority and the bodies of local self-government, as well as the officials thereof shall provide to each citizen access to any documents and materials directly affecting his/her rights and liberties unless otherwise stipulated under the law.

273. The above principles are detailed in the LC. Employee data which has to be protected is recognized as information necessary to the employer in connection with labour relations and pertaining to a particular employee. A request about an employee's personal details from any third party, as well as the use of such information, is allowed only with the prior written consent of the employee. Employers are obliged to protect employees' personal information and must notify each employee about the internal procedure for its storage, use and protection.

To ensure the rights and liberties of a human being and citizen, the employer and his/her representatives must observe the following general requirements in the processing of employees' personal data:

(a) the employer must inform the employee of the goals, expected sources and methods of getting personal data, as well as of the nature of the expected personal data and the consequences of employee refusal to give the written consent to get them;
(b) the employer may not obtain and process employee personal data of special spheres (such as on her/his political, religious and other convictions and private

91. *See* paras 87 and 88.

life, or membership in public associations or his/her trade union activities, except in the cases envisaged in federal law;

(c) employees and their representatives must be acknowledged against receipt with the documents of the organization setting forth the procedure of processing of employee personal data, as well as with their rights and duties in this sphere; and

(d) employers, employees and their representatives must work out jointly the measures of protection of employee personal data.

274. Employees have the right to receive full information on their personal data and processing of these data; the right to have free unpaid access to own personal data including the right to get a copy of any record containing employee personal data, except for the cases envisaged in the federal law; and the right to appeal in court against any illegal actions or failure to act of the employer in the processing and protection of his/her personal data.

Chapter 3. Working Time, Annual Vacations and Holidays (Including Overtime and Sunday Duty)

§1. Working Time

I. The Notion

275. The current LC contains the notion of working time. In particular Article 91 of the RF LC reads that working time is the period of time during which an employee in accordance with the rules of internal labour order of the organization and an employment contract must perform labour duties.

Working time also includes other periods in compliance with laws and other normative legal acts. In particular such periods include established interruptions during work (such as breaks for rest, meal or warming; and breaks for women for child feeding).

276. The aspects of working time are regulated both by state and local (by employers) levels. Legislation on working time consists of the RF LC, laws containing rules about working time for certain categories of workers, as well as of secondary legislation – mostly acts of the Government of the RF, the adoption of which is often prescribed by the LC. For example, peculiarities of working time regime and rest time of employees of transport, communications and other services having a special nature of work are determined according to the procedure established by the Government of the RF.

II. Normal (Standard) Working Time

277. Russian LL refers to several types of working time. The standard (so-called normal) duration of working time may not exceed forty hours per week.

The duration of working time for a particular employee can be increased in accordance with some types of collective agreements and under her/his written consent (Article 92).

III. Reduced Working Time

278. The normal duration of working time may be limited. Reduced time is established for special categories of employees. Mostly reduced working time is stated by legislation (by the LC of the RF or by other federal laws) and covers the following categories of employees:

(1) employees up to 16 years of age 18 – 24 hours per week;[92]

---

92. *See also* para. 427.

(2) employees from 16 to 18 years of age – 35 hours per week (this was changed in 2006);[93]
(3) disabled workers (of 1 and 2 degree of invalidity) – 35 hours per week;
(4) employees engaged in works with harmful and/or dangerous conditions – 36 hours per week (the list of appropriate works is established by the Government of the RF); and
(5) teaching personnel of educational institutions – 36 hours per week;[94] medical workers – the number of working hours is set to the limit of not more than 39 hours a week. Depending on a position and (or) type of work, the number of working hours for medical workers is defined by the Government of the RF.

Regarding some categories of employees the reduced working time is stated by laws (e.g., employees involved in works with chemical weapons and miners).

279. The RF LC establishes the limited duration of daily working time. In particular the duration of daily working time cannot exceed:

(a) 4 hours – for employees of 14–15 years of age; 5 hours – for employees of 15–16 years of age;
(b) 7 hours – regarding employees of 16–18 years of age;
(c) for disabled employees – according to the results of medical examination; and
(d) for employees involved in dangerous or harmful environments – 8 hours (in case of a 36-hour working week); 6 hours (regarding a 30-hour (or less) working week).

280. Reduced working time may be also established by employment contracts, as well as collective agreements. Both collective and individual employment contracts may limit the work of females employed in the Far North regions and equivalent areas to 36 hours per week.[95]

281. It should be noted that reduced working time is paid on the same rates as for full working week. This rule does not apply regarding workers under 18 years of age who are paid taking into account short workday. Of course, the employer may effect additional payments to them up to appropriate job payment rates for full workday at his own expense.

IV. Non-full Working Time (Part-time Work)

282. In general, part-time work may be established by the agreement between the employee and the employer at anytime. Regarding certain employees (such as pregnant women, one of the parents with a child under 14 years of age (disabled

93. The duration of working time for some categories of students up to 18 years, which are involved in work during the period of study, may not exceed half of the norm specified above.
94. Article 333 of the RF LC.
95. Article 320 of the RF LC.

child – under 18 years of age), as well as the person taking care of the sick member of the family as specified in the medical statement), the employer is obliged to establish part-time work at their request.

283. Sometimes non-full working time may be applied at the employer's initiative. Such situations are recognized as transformation of the employment contract (changing of its significant conditions) and shall be madein accordance with the rules required. In particular Article 73 of the LC proves the right of an employer to initiate changes of significant conditions of a contract of employment because of reasons connected with change of organizational or technological aspects of job environment if the labour function (agreed type of work) of employee is not changed. At the same time, the employee must be informed about these changes by the employer in written form no less than two month prior to their enactment. If the employee engaged does not agree to continue working in the new environment, then the employer must offer a different existing job position to an employee in written form. This position must correspond to qualification and state of health according to the results of medical examination of employee. If such a position does not exist then the employer must offer the employee a lower position with job functions that the employee can perform according to his/her qualification and state of health according to the results of medical examination. If such a job position does not exist and if the employee rejects an offered position then the contract of employment is terminated according to paragraph 7 of Article 77 of the LC.

284. As distinct from reduced working time, with a part-time work arrangement, the earnings to the employee are paid in proportion to the working time or depending on the fulfilled volume of work.

§2. Night Work

285. Under LL, night-time is recognized as the period from 22.00 to 6.00 (Article 96 of the LC).

There is a general rule that the duration of working time (shift) at night is reduced by one hour. This rule does not apply to employees to whom the reduced working time is established,[96] if anything different is not specified in a collective agreement.

286. It is prohibited to employ some categories of people to work at night (e.g., pregnant women, disabled employees, employees under 18 years of age, with the exception of entities involved in creation and (or) performance of pieces of art and some others).

Women, who have children under three years of age; employees who have disabled children;employees responsible for nursing disabled members of their families according to results of medical examination; mothers and fathers who have growing children below the age of 5 without a matrimonial partner; and guardians of children of the indicated age can be allowed to work at night only with their

96. *See* paras 285–287.

written confirmation and if this kind of work is not forbidden to them because of their state of health according to medical examination. These employees must be informed in written form about their right to refuse working at night.

§3. Work on Days off and Holidays

287. All employees are granted days off (weekly continuous rest). For a five-day working week, employees are given two days off a week, and in the case of six-day working week, they are given one day off.

Sunday is a common day off. The other day off in case of a five-day working week is established by the collective agreement or by the internal labour regulations of the organization. Both days off are given successively, as a rule.[97]

288. The list of holidays is provided by the RF LC.[98] It includes the following non-working holidays:

(a) 1–6, 8 January – New Year Holidays;
(b) 7 January – Christmas;
(c) 23 February – the Day of the Defendant of Motherland;
(d) 8 March – the International Women's Day;
(e) 1 May – the Spring and Labour Holiday;
(f) 9 May – the Victory Day;
(g) 12 June – the Day of Russia; and
(h) 4 November – the Day of Unity of Population.

289. If a day off coincides with a non-working holiday, the day offis shifted as a rule to the working day which follows the holiday. The Government of the RF has the right to shift days off to other days so that employees could use their days off and non-working holidays more rationally.

290. Russian LL has a general rule that reads that work on days off, as well as on non-working holidays, is prohibited. Exceptions may occur only in some exclusive cases (such as need for work for purposes of prevention or elimination of social distress or natural catastrophe, industrial accident or immediate elimination of their consequences; for implementation of urgent and unforeseen works, from which promptness fulfilment the further normal operation of enterprise, institution, organization as a whole or their separate subdivisions shall depend and so on).

The work on the day off shall be compensated by granting another day off or, under agreement of parties, in monetary mode, but at least at twofold rate.

§4. Work Beyond the Normal (Standard) Working Time

291. Working beyond the limits of normal length of working time can be performed in the following cases:

97. Article 111 of the RF LC.
98. Article 112 of the RF LC.

(a) on the initiative of the employee – off-time work (secondary employment or doing multiple jobs); and
(b) on the initiative of the employer (overtime).

I. Off-time Work

292. Off-time work is the carrying out of other paid work (several works) by an employee under a contract (contracts) of employment. This work is done in his/her free time. An employment contract on off-time work may be concluded with an unlimited number of employers if the federal law does not stipulate another procedure. The employee may execute off-work both on his (her) principal place of work, as well as in other organizations.

The RF LC has a special chapter regulating other particulars of legal status of employees engaged in the above works.

293. Off-time work is restricted for employees under 18 years of age, as well as for hard work and work under unhealthy and/or dangerous conditions if their principal job is also carried out under similar conditions. Regarding some categories of workers, the involvement in this type of work is limited by legislation (e.g., leading personnel).

294. It is necessary to mention that work beyond normal limits of working time on the conditions above cannot exceed four hours per day. For some categories of employee, this limitation may be increased (in particular for medical workers, employed in public health care organizations, who live and work in rural areas and small towns, the number of working hours available for dual jobholding can be increased in accordance with state regulations).

II. Overtime Work

295. Overtime work is defined as that performed by an employee on the initiative of employer beyond the limits of normal length of working time, daily working time (shift) and working more than normal number of hours in a recorded period without conclusion of additional contract of employment. Overtime work cannot exceed 4 hours in 2 days and 120 hours in a year for each employee. An employer must precisely record all overtime work performed by each employee.

296. Overtime work is allowed only in a limited number of instances. Upon the written consent of an employee, overtime work may be performed in the cases specified on the LC as listed below:

(1) to complete work that could not be completed in normal working time as a result of an unexpected delay because of technological reasons, if non-completion of this work may lead to damage or destruction of employer's property, state or municipal property or may cause danger to life and health of people, etc.
(2) when temporary works on repairing and restoring of damaged machines or buildings are performed, if malfunctioning or damage may lead to stopping of work for a large number of employees, etc.[99]

The RF LC refers to situations when overtime work is allowed without the written consent of an employee (e.g., when it is necessary for the defence of the country or for the prevention of industrial accidents).

In cases which are not stipulated by the RF LC, overtime work is allowed only with the consideration of the opinion of the elected trade union authority of the organization and with the consent of the employee.

297. It is not allowed to request overtime work from pregnant women, workers below the age of 18 years and other categories of employees according to federal laws. Requesting overtime work from invalids and women who have children below the age of 3 is allowed only with their written consent and if these works are not forbidden to do so because of state of health according to the results of medical examination. Invalids and women who have children below the age of 3 must be informed in written form about their right to refuse working overtime.

§5. Working Time Regime

298. The working time regime provides the distribution of working days during the working week. Therefore different regimes (e.g., five-day week with two days off, six-day week with one day off, flexible schedule of days off, irregular (non-fixed) working day, etc.) may be established.

As a rule the regime of work is specified in local legal acts of an employer, as well as in collective agreements and individual employment contracts. But some aspects of working time regime are defined by legislation. In particular the LC makes a reference that particulars of the working time and rest time regime of the employees of transportation, communication and other spheres with the work of specific nature shall be defined according to the procedure fixed by the Government of the RF.

I. Irregular (Non-fixed) Regime

299. For some categories of employees, a so-called irregular (or non-fixed) working regime may be established. Irregular working time is defined as a special work routine when some individual employees may be involved in their labour

99. Article 99 of the RF LC.

function fulfilment episodically beyond the standard working hours as ordered by the employer from necessity. The RF LC granted employers the right to list professions with no fixed working hours and develop internal regulations in relation thereto.[100] In particular the list of employees engaged may be determined by collective agreement, as well as other internal labour regulations of the organization, issued with taking into account the opinion of representatives of employees.

II. Flexible Working Regime

300. As distinct from the irregular regime, a flexible working regime means that the beginning, the end or the total duration of working hours is determined by the parties' agreement. The employer ensures that the employee should work the total number of working hours within the appropriate record-keeping periods (a working day, week, month and others).[101]

III. Work in Shifts

301. Working in shifts is another type of working regime. It is introduced in cases when the duration of the production process exceeds the permissible length of daily work, as well as for the purposes of more efficient use of equipment, increase of the volume of produced output or rendered services. With the shift work arrangement, each of the groups of employees must fulfil the work within specified length of the working time according to the shift schedule. Shift operation schedules are to be brought to the notice of employees not later than one month before their carrying into effect. To work two shifts running is banned.[102] In such cases working time is summed up in accordance with the rules prescribed by the LC (Article 104).

IV. Dividing of Working Time into Parts

302. In certain types of work, where it is necessary due to the special nature of labour as well as in executing work of different intensity during the working day (shift), the working day can be divided into parts, so that the total duration of working hours does not exceed the established duration of the daily work. This division is carried out by the employer on the basis of the local standard act, adopted with taking into account the opinion of the elected trade union body of the given organization. Such rules are for instance applied to transport workers.

---

100. Article 101 of the RF LC.
101. Article 102 of the RF LC. *See also* 'Recommendations on Applying the Flexible Working Time Regime at Enterprises or in Organizations of Branches of National Economy' approved by the Decision of the State Committee of the USSR for Issues of Labour and Wages and Secretariat of the All-Union Central Council of Trade Unions No. 162/12–55 of 30 May 1985 and 'The List of Workers of Communication for Whom the Flexible Working Regime May Be Established' approved by The Order of the RF Ministry of Communication of 8 Sep. 2003 No. 112.
102. Article 103 of the RF LC.

§6. ANNUAL PAID LEAVE

303. In accordance with the RF Constitution, everyone has the right to rest (Article 37). The RF LC[103] provides the list of types of rest time guaranteed by labour legislation for all employees, without dependency on types of enterprises. Besides breaks during the working day, days off and non-working holidays, the rest time includes the leaves.

I. Regular Annual Paid Leave

304. The RF LC provides for twenty-eight calendar days of paid vacation per annum (the leave). Generally, an employee is entitled to vacation after six months from the time his/her employment commenced.

Regarding some categories of employees, the duration of annual leaves is more than the above period. In particular workers under the age of 18 years are entitled to annual paid leave of 31 calendar days.[104] Teachers also have the right to such prolonged leave.[105]

II. Additional Annual Paid Leave

305. The RF LC envisages mandatory additional leave for employees working in certain industries and those with no fixed working hours. For instance, employees occupied with works with harmful working conditions, occupied in some branches of national economy and having a long record of service at one enterprise, employees with an unlimited working day, employees working in the Far North regions and equivalent regions. Usually additional paid leave is summed up with regular annual paid leave.

306. Additional annual paid leave is provided to the following categories of employees:

- engaged in the works with adverse and/or hazardous working conditions (such as in underground mining works and opencast mining works, in radioactive contamination zones and in other works associated with irremovable adverse impact on the human health of harmful physical, chemical, biological and other factors);
- having a special nature of work (e.g., doctors and teaching personnel);
- having irregular working day; and
- working in the regions of the Far North and similar localities.

103. Article 107 of the RF LC.
104. Article 267 of the RF LC.
105. *See* the Order of the RF Federal Agency of Education of 27 Feb. 2007 No. 405 'On Duration of Annual Paid Leave for Pedagogical Workers'; *see also* 'Decision of the RF Government of 1 Oct. 2002 No. 724 "On Duration of Prolonged Paid Annual Leaves for Teachers"'.

Employers, taking into account their production and financial resources, may institute additional leave for their employees if otherwise is not envisaged in the federal laws. The procedure and terms of providing this leave shall be defined in the collective agreement or the local normative acts.

307. Employees with an irregular working day should be provided with additional annual paid leave, with the length being defined in the collective agreement or internal work rules. Such a leave may not be shorter than three calendar days. If such leave is not provided, the work in excess of the standard length of the working time shall be compensated as overtime work if the employee agrees to it.[106]

308. According to Article 173 of the LC, workers who are successfully studying in the state accredited institutions of higher education by correspondence or at evening courses are entitled to additional paid leave in order to:

(a) pass tests and exams (forty calendar days each for the fifty and second courses; fifty calendar days for each course that follows);
(b) prepare and defend a diploma thesis (project) – four months and so on.

III. The Procedure for Granting Paid Leave

309. The procedure for granting annual paid leave is defined in general by the LC. The priority of granting annual paid leave is established annually in accordance with the schedule of leave, which is to be approved by the employer, considering the opinion of the elected trade union body of the given organization, not later than two weeks before the beginning of the calendar year.

310. Realization of the right to annual paid leave depends on the employee's length of service in the appropriate organization.[107] The length of service providing the right for the regular annual paid leave includes time of actual work; time when the employee actually did not work but preserved the place of work (position) according to the federal laws including the time of the annual paid leave; time of involuntary absence in case of unlawful dismissal or removal from work followed by subsequent reinstatement in the previous job; and other periods of time envisaged in the collective agreement, a contract of employment, as well as in local normative act of the employer. Some periods are not included into the length of service (e.g., time of absence of the employee without justifiable reasons; and time of established childcare leaves). The length of service providing the right for the additional annual paid leaves for the work with adverse and/or hazardous working conditions shall include only the time actually spent under the respective conditions.

106. Article 119 of the RF LC. *See also* 'The Rules of Granting of an Additional Paid Leave for Workers Engaged in Irregular Working Day in Organizations Financed by the Federal Budget' approved by the Decision of the RF Government No. 884 of 11 Dec. 2002.
107. Article 121 of the RF LC.

311. Paid leave must be provided to the employee on the annual basis. The right for the use of the leave for the first year of work begins for the employee upon expiry of six months of his/her uninterrupted work in the given organization. If there is an agreement between the parties, the paid leave to the employee may be provided before expiry of the six months. Moreover, before the expiry of the above six months of uninterrupted work, the paid leave at the employee application must be provided to women before their pregnancy leave or directly after it; to employees up to 18 years of age; to employees having adopted a child (children) up to 3 months of age; and in other cases envisaged in the federal laws.

312. Some categories of employees are granted their annual paid leave according to their wish at the time suitable for them in cases provided for by federal laws. For instance, a husband may be given his annual paid leave by his request during his wife's maternity leave, regardless the period of his continuous work in the given organization. *See also* paragraph 421.

313. It is banned not to grant the annual paid leave for two successive years, as well as not to grant annual paid leave to employees under 18 years of age and employees involved in work with harmful and (or) dangerous labour conditions.

314. Under the agreement between the employer and the employee, annual paid leave may be divided into parts. In this case at least one of the parts of this leave cannot be shorter than fourteen calendar days.[108]

IV. Replacing Annual Paid Leave with Monetary Compensation

315. The part of the leave exceeding twenty-eight calendar days may be replaced with money compensation on employee's written application. It is not allowed to replace the leave with money compensation to expectant mothers and employees under 18 years of age, as well as to employees involved in hard work and work with harmful and (or) dangerous labour conditions (except cases stipulated by the LC). At the dismissal the employee is paid money compensation for all unused leave.

§7. Unpaid Leave

316. Under family circumstances or for other good reasons the employee may be given, on the written request, leave without pay, the duration of which is determined under the agreement between the employee and the employer.[109]

317. Employees who combine their work with education are also entitled to receive leave without pay for the following purposes:

108. Article 125 of the RF LC.
109. Article 128 of the RF LC.

(a) to pass entry exams to institutions of higher education – ten calendar days;
(b) to take preparatory courses for entry exams to institutions of higher education – fifteen calendar days; and
(c) to study in institutions of higher education on day course basis, combining studies with work (for passing tests and exams – ten calendar days per academic year; for preparing and defending diploma thesis (project) – two months, and for passing graduate exams – one month and some others.

318. In some cases an employer is obliged to provide unpaid leave upon the written request of the employee. The following unpaid leave is provided for the categories of employees listed below:

(a) participants of the Great Patriotic War (World War II) – up to thirty-five calendar days during a year;
(b) retired workers receiving old-age pension – up to fourteen calendar days during a year;
(c) parents and wives (husbands) of military personnel, killed or dead owing to wounding, contusion or mutilation got while acting as military, or owing to a disease concerned with doing military service – up to fourteen calendar days during a year;
(d) working disabled people – up to sixty calendar days during a year;
(e) employees in cases of a child birth, wedding registration and death of close relatives – up to five calendar days.

Other cases may be stated by federal laws, as well as collective agreements (Article 128 of the LC).

Chapter 4. Remuneration and Benefits

§1. The Notion of Remuneration

319. Previously the Russian LC made reference to the two following notions regarding the current topic. Remuneration itself was understood as a system of relations concerned with the employer's establishment and provision of payments to employees for their labour in accordance with laws, other standard legal acts, collective agreements, local standard acts and labour contracts. Salary (or wages) is recognized as a reward for labour depending on the employee's qualifications, as well as the amount, quality and terms of work fulfilled. The latter also included payments of compensation and incentive payments (bonuses, premiums).[110] It should be noted that the current LC uses the above-mentioned notion of salary (or wages).

320. The main characteristics of remuneration as part of the employment relationship are as follows:

(a) It is one of the basic rights of workers to be paid wages timely and in full in accordance with qualification, complexity of work and its quantity and quality.
(b) As a rule, wages are paid in a monetary form.
(c) Remuneration is stated in accordance with established tariffs with taking into account the worker's labour contribution.
(d) It is not limited by maximum amount (if otherwise is not prescribed by legislation), but may not be lower than the established minimum.[111]

§2. The Regulation of Remuneration

321. According to the Article 37 of the RF Constitution, every citizen has the right to equal pay without discrimination. The principle of equal pay for equal work is also stated by Russian labour legislation.

Remuneration for each employee's labour depends on his/her personal labour contribution and quality of labour.

322. The significant feature of the employment relationship is a specific method of establishing wages. The regulation of remuneration is represented by several levels. For employees of the budget-financed companies, the system of wages, as well as the base wage rates and different kinds of payments, is established by appropriate laws and other legal acts.

The wage establishing for the employees of the companies with mixed financing (budget financing and revenues from business activities) is undertaken by laws, other standard legal acts, local legal acts, as well as by contracts (both collective agreements and individual employment contracts). As concerns employees engaged

110. Article 129 of the RF LC.
111. Khnikin, G.V., 'Zarabotnaya Plata', in: *Labour Law of Russia* (Textbook), Moscow: Moscow State University, 'Jurist', 2004, p. 285.

in the relationships with private companies, all aspects of remuneration are regulated by collective agreements, other local acts of the company, as well as by individual employment contracts.

As follows from the above, state intervention in regulation of remuneration is mostly felt in the sphere of budget-financed organizations (companies). At the same time, it should be noted that the scope of local regulation of remuneration has been enlarged in recent years.

323. State regulation of remuneration also establishes minimum guarantees in this sphere. The system of main state guarantees of remuneration of labour to employees includes:

(1) the amount of the minimum wage in the RF;
(2) the amount of the minimum base wage rate of employees of budget-financed organizations in the RF;
(3) measures to provide a higher level of the real wage content;
(4) protection of wages (e.g., limiting of the list of grounds and amounts of deductions from wages under the employer's order, as well as the amount of taxation of incomes on the base of wages);
(5) limitations regarding remuneration in kind;
(6) providing for the employee to receive wages in case of the employer's cessation of activities and his or her insolvency in accordance with federal laws;
(7) state supervision and control of complete and timely payment of wages and realization of state guarantees of remuneration of labour;
(8) the employers' responsibility for infringement of requirements, stipulated by legislation, as well as by collective agreements; and
(9) terms and the order of priority in paying wages.

324. The monthly wage of an employee who has completely fulfilled working time standards (labour rates) and performed his/her labour duties cannot be lower than the minimum wage stipulated by law.

The current LC requires that the minimum wage cannot be lower than the amount of the subsistence level (cost of living of an able-bodied person).[112] But this provision of the LC is not in force until a special federal law will be issued to this effect. In recent years this amount has been regularly increased, but it is still not in accordance with the subsistence level.

325. The minimum wage amount is established simultaneously on the whole territory of the RF. At the same time, henceforth the minimal wage set at the federal level is financed from the Federal Budget (in the organizations financed by the Federal Budget); from the budgets of the subjects of the RF (in the organizations financed by the budgets of the subjects of the RF); in the organizations backed by the local budgets it is financed from the local budgets; and in other organizations from their own funds.

---

112. Article 133 of the RF LC.

The subjects of the RF may issue their laws establishing the minimum wage within the territory of the appropriate subject.

326. Wages are to be paid in the monetary form in the currency of the RF (roubles), if otherwise is not defined by the LC. Collective agreements or contracts of employment can envisage other forms of wage payments, if this does not contradict federal law or international treaties entered into by the RF. The amount of non-monetary wage payments cannot exceed 20% of the total amount of wages.[113]

327. Article 134 of the RF LC provides for wage indexation. For budget-financed enterprises, the procedure for indexation is established by law; for profit-financed enterprises, this procedure is established in collective agreements and other local legal acts.

328. Wages are to be paid at least once in every two weeks.[114] The compensation for annual paid vacation must be paid at least three days prior to the vacation date. A particular date is usually defined in local normative acts as well as collective agreements or follows from individual contracts.

§3. Pay Systems

329. The system of remuneration and encouragement of labour, including payment rise for working at nights, at weekends and on non-working holidays, payment for overtime work and other cases is established by the employer considering the opinion of the elected trade union body of this company.

I. Tariff System of Remuneration

330. The tariff system is an aggregate of standards, which are used to differentiate salaries or wages of different categories of employees.

The tariff system of remuneration includes: base wage rates (salaries), tariff scale and tariff coefficients. The basic wage (rate) is a fixed remuneration of labour of an employee for fulfilment of the labour duties of a definite complexity (qualifications) for a time unit. The tariff scale is an aggregate of wage categories of work (professions, posts), defined depending on the work complexity and the employee's skill characteristics with the help of tariff coefficients.

331. The complexity of operations to be fulfilled is definedon the basis of their rating. Work rating and the awarding of wage categories to the employee is donein accordance with the *Common Rate Book for Work and Workers' Jobs*, the *Common*

113. Article 131 of the LC.
114. Article 136 of the LC.

Qualification Book of Posts for Executives, Specialists and Clerks. These books and rules of their usage are approved in accordance with the procedure established by the Government of the RF.

332. The tariff system of remuneration for the employees of organizations financed from budgets of all levels is established on the basis of the common tariff scale for remuneration of labour of budgetary worker which is approved in accordance with the procedure established by the federal law and which is the guarantee of remuneration of labour of budgetary workers.

The tariff system of remuneration is not obligatory for employees engaged in the private sector of economy. But it can be accepted in accordance with collective agreements and oriented as stated by legislation characteristics of professional qualification groups (Article 144 of the LC).

II. Incentive Payments (Bonuses, Premiums)

333. An employer has the right to establish different premium systems, extra incentive payments and allowances considering the opinion of the employees' representative body. The above-mentioned systems may be established by collective agreements as well. The procedure and terms of using stimulating and compensating payments (extra payments, premiums, allowances) in the organizations financed from the Federal Budget are defined by the Government of the RF; in organizations financed from the budget of a subject of the RF, they are defined by the bodies of state power of this subject of the RF; and in the organizations financed from the local budget, they are defined by the bodies of local self-management.[115]

§4. Remuneration on Special Conditions

I. Remuneration of Employees Involved in Dangerous Work

334. Remuneration of employees involved in hard work, in work with harmful and (or) dangerous and other special labour conditions is made in increased amounts as compared to base wage rates (salaries) established for various jobs with standard labour conditions. The minimum amounts are defined by legislation. A list of such dangerous works is issued by the RF Government.[116]

II. Work in Special Climatic Conditions

335. Remuneration in special climatic conditions (e.g., the Far North) is made in accordance with the procedure and at amounts not lower than those defined by legislation.

---

115. Article 144 of the RF LC.
116. Article 147 of the RF LC.

III. Performance of Work Requiring Different Qualifications

336. When the employee with payment per hour performs work of different qualifications, he/she is paid as for the work requiring the higher qualifications. When the employee with a piece-rate pay performs work of different qualifications, he/she is paid at the rates of the work he/she performs. In cases when considering the type of production the employee with a piece-rate pay is requested to perform work rated lower than his/her awarded grade, the employer is obliged to pay the difference between the grades.[117]

IV. Performance of the Duties of a Temporarily Absent Employee

337. An employee who performs, along with his/her main job stipulated by the employment contract, an additional job (post), or performs the duties of an employee who is temporarily away from work, without being relieved of his/her main post is paid extra for combining jobs (posts) or for performing the duties of a temporarily absent employee. The amount of extra pay is established on the agreement of the parties of the employment contract with taking into account the volume of additional work (Article 60.2 of the LC).[118]

V. Overtime

338. Russian legislation complies with the requirements of international rules (including the European Social Charter) in stating the right of the workforce to receive overtime pay. At the same time, experience shows that employers frequently expand the use of overtime without always observing minimal guarantees on overtime pay. This practice is particularly widespread at times of high unemployment.

Payment for overtime work should be half as much again for the first two hours of work not less than at twofold rate for the subsequent hours. The particular amount of the payment may be defined by the collective agreement or the employment contract. At the employee's request, instead of an increased payment his/her overtime work may be compensated by granting additional time for rest but not less than the time worked out overtime.[119]

VI. Payments for Work on Days off and Non-working Holidays

339. Work on a day off and on a non-working holiday is to be paid not less than twice the normal amount. According to the wish of the employee who worked on a

117. Article 150 of the RF LC.
118. Article 151 of the RF LC.
119. Article 152 of the RF LC, *see also* paras 302–304.

day off or on a non-working holiday, he may be given another day off. In this case the work on a non-working holiday is paid at the single rate, but the day off is not paid.[120]

Remuneration of labour on days off and on non-working holidays of creative workers of organizations of cinematography, theatres, theatre and concert organizations, circuses and other individuals taking part in the creation and (or) performing works of art, professional sportsmen in accordance with the list of professions defined by the Government of the RF considering the opinion of RTC adjustment, may be defined on the basis of the employment contract, collective agreement or other local act.[121]

VII. Night Work

340. Every hour of work at night is to be paid in the increased amount as compared to the work in normal conditions. The amount of the increase is defined by the employer considering the opinion of the employees' representative body, collective agreement and contract of employment. Regarding some categories of employees they are stated by legislation.[122]

VIII. Remuneration if Labour Rates Are Not Fulfilled

341. Labour norms (rates) – standard output, time, servicing norms – are established for employees in accordance with the achieved level of engineering, technology, organization of production and labour. Labour norms may be revised as they improve or new equipment and technologies are introduced, organizational or other measures providing an increased productivity are conducted, as well as in case of using worn-out and obsolete equipment.

Local normative acts providing the introduction, change and revision of labour norms are to be accepted by the employer considering the opinion of the employees' representative body. Employees must be informed about the introduction of new labour norms not later than two months ahead.[123]

342. When the established labour norms (rates) are not fulfilled through the employer's fault, payment is made for actually worked out time or the work done but not less than the average wages of the employee calculated for the same period of time or for the work done. When labour rates are not fulfilled for reasons which do not depend on the employer and employee, at least two-thirds of the base wage

120. Article 153 of the RF LC.
121. *See also* paras 294–297.
122. *See also* paras 292 and 293.
123. Articles 160–162 of the RF LC.

rate is reserved for the employee. When labour rates are not fulfilled through the employee's fault, payment of the rated part of wages is made in accordance with the amount of work done.[124]

IX. Payment of Downtime

343. Downtime (temporary stopping of work) through the employer's fault (if the employee informed the employer in writing about the beginning of the downtime) is paid in the amount of not less than two-thirds of the employee's average wages. Downtime through the employee's fault is not paid.[125]

§5. Protection of Remuneration

344. Russian LL follows international rules concerning protection in the sphere of work payments (the ILO Convention N95). The RF LC contains guarantees to protect employees' pay from arbitrary reductions, in particular by providing lists of permissible reductions and defining their limits. Deductions from wages can be made only in the cases envisaged in the LC and other federal laws. According to Article 137 of the LC, wage deductions with a view to setting off workers' indebtedness against the employer may be effectuated in the following cases:

(1) to be paid back for an advance payment on work that the worker failed to perform;
(2) to pay off an advance payment made to the worker going on a business trip or being transferred to another location, or for any economic expenses associated therewith, that was not spent or not returned in due time;
(3) to return any extra amounts paid to the worker as a result of accounting mistakes; and
(4) to compensate for days taken as vacation, if the worker is dismissed prior to the end of the working year and he/she has already used up his/her annual vacation leave. No money shall be withheld for these days if the employee is being dismissed for the definite reasons (such as staff reduction).

With each payment of wages, the total amount of all deductions shall not exceed 20%, while in the cases specifically envisaged by federal law the latter may amount to 50%. If wage deduction is made according to several executive documents, the worker by all means retains 50% of his/her wage (Article 138 of the LC).

345. The RF LC obliges employers to pay employees compensation for each day of delay in payment of wages and other employment-related payments. The amount of such compensation may not be less than 1/300 of the effective Central Bank refinancing rate.

124. Article 155 of the RF LC.
125. Article 157 of the RF LC.

Legislation on bankruptcy (in particular, the RF Law 'On Bankruptcy') recognizes the employee's privilege to receive wages – not only in the event of bankruptcy, but also when the employer has cash-flow problems.

346. In case of delay in payment for the period exceeding fifteen days, having submitted a written notification to the employer, the employee has the right to suspend work for the whole period until the payment of the delayed sum. Suspension of work is not allowed in the following situations:

(a) during the period of introducing the state of emergency, martial law or special measures in accordance with the laws on the state of emergency;
(b) in bodies and organizations of the armed forces of the RF, other military, militarized and other units and organizations responsible for the country defence and security of the state, doing rescue and fire prevention operations, work on prevention or liquidations of natural disasters and emergency situations and in law enforcement bodies;
(c) in organizations directly servicing extremely dangerous types of production and equipment; and
(d) in organizations connected with the provision of vital activity for people (power supply, central heating, water supply, gas supply, communications, ambulance and first aid).

The above legal requirements are taken into account in legislation on bankruptcy, as well as in tax legislation (Article 226 of the RF Tax Code).

Chapter 5. Incapacity to Work

347. The legal rules concerning incapacity to work follow from the assumption that an employer bears the appropriate risks. As a rule an employer is responsible for making payments established by the legislation in case of incapacity (excluding the incapacity to work caused by the employee's fault). Some situations of incapacity demand that an employer reserve the place of working.

In general it is banned to dismiss (except in cases of liquidation of the organization or termination of activities of the employer out of natural persons) during the period of temporary disability of the employee, as well as during the period of his/her leave.

§1. Incapacity Caused by Worker's Fault

348. If an employee does not fulfil the labour duties, an employer may apply disciplinary penalties. Among these penalties is termination of an employment contract (dismissal) which may be undertaken in cases stipulated by legislation. For instance, an employee may be dismissed in case of repeated non-fulfilment of job functions, as well as if he/she made a single violation of job duties. The list of such single violations as grounds for dismissal is established by legislation and includes, for instance, absence from work without reasonable excuse for a period longer than four consequent hours during a working day.[126]

349. Sometimes an employer is obliged to make payments when the established labour rates (functions) are not fulfilled by an employee. Regarding such cases there may be several possibilities. But when it happens because of the fault of an employee, an employer is not obliged to pay full amount of the agreed wage.[127]

§2. Incapacity to Work Caused by the Health of an Employee

I. Temporary Disability

350. When the employee is prevented from working because of illness that is recognized as a temporary disability, the employer may not terminate a contract of employment.

According to Russian legislation, employees (and in appropriate cases their families) are provided with benefits of temporary disability. The obligation of an employer is to provide such insurance (which means – to pay taxes to state budget, as well as social insurance contributions to the special social funds for the purposes of compulsory social insurance). The appropriate benefits are paid to employees

126. *See also* paras 387–389.
127. *See also* paras 348 and 349.

through the financial department of an employer (and finally reimbursed by the appropriate state financial funds, such as for instance RF SIF).[128]

II. Industrial Accidents and Professional Diseases

351. In case of damage of health of an employee (or death) resulted from industrial accident or professional disease, the employee (in case of death – his/her family) is to be paid the lost earnings (income), as well as extra costs for medical social and professional rehabilitation associated with the health damage (or the appropriate costs in view of the employee's death). Types, amounts and terms of granting guarantees and compensations in these cases are defined by social security legislation (in particular, by legal acts on obligatory social insurance against professional risks). *See* paragraph 96.

An employer is obliged to investigate every industrial accident. For these purposes the employer shall immediately create a commission consisting of no fewer than three persons. The appropriate procedure is established by the RF LC.[129]

III. Pregnancy and Childcare

352. Upon the request and in accordance with medical reports, females are to be granted maternity leave.[130] During this leave women receive maternity benefits in accordance with social security legislation.[131] Therefore the benefits are financed by the state, while as a rule they are paid by an employer (e.g., through the financial department).

353. Pregnancy itself may not be the reason to terminate a contract on the initiative of an employer. An employment contract with a pregnant woman may be terminated only in cases stipulated by legislation (e.g., liquidation of organization).[132]

354. An employer is obliged to keep the previous level of wages in cases of changing of employment with pregnant women. Labour rates and service standards may be reduced for a pregnant female employee in accordance with a medical report and upon her request. Such employees may be moved to another job (excluding one with unfavourable working environment) with reservation of average wage. Before making a decision about moving a pregnant female to another job, she is to be released from her previous job and the employer is to pay her average salary for all days missed due to this procedure. The average salary for the pregnant female is also reserved for the period of obligatory medical examination.

128. *See* paras 102–104.
129. Articles 228–230 of the RF LC.
130. Regarding its duration *see* para. 418, item 4.
131. *See* paras 99–101.
132. *See* para. 418, item 3.

Sometimes the obligation to reserve the same wage concerns women who have children under 18 months of age. If such women are not able to perform the previous work, they should be moved to another job upon their request with reservation of their average salary up to time when their child reaches the age of 18 months.[133]

355. Upon the request of a female employee, she is granted a childcare leave up to when her child reaches the age of 3 years. The procedure and terms of social payments during the above-mentioned leave are specified by social security legislation.[134] The employer's obligation is limited by keeping the opportunity for the woman to return to her work at any time during the leave. It should be also noted that such leaves may be granted in full or partially to the child's father, grandmother, grandfather, other relatives or tutor actually nursing the child. Some aspects of applying of the legislation on work performed by women, as well as by persons with family responsibilities are detailed by the Decision of the RF Supreme Court of 28 January 2014 N1.

IV. Invalidity

356. When an employer is recognized as able to work only partly (or not be able to work completely), he/she receives the status of a disabled person (an invalid). This status is provided by the state bodies of medical-social expertise.

Invalidity itself may not be the ground for termination of a contract of employment. The RF LC provides an employer with the opportunity to dismiss a disabled person only if an employee is not fit for the occupied position or performed job functions because of state of health according to medical examination. Before such dismissal an employer is obliged to suggest other work to be done by the disabled employee (in accordance with his/her state of health). Therefore, if a disabled employee is shifted to another position, he/she must be compensated in remuneration. In particular, the RF LC states that when transferring the employee to another permanent less paid job in connection with the medical certificate stating that he/she needs another job, his/her previous average wages are preserved for the period of one month from the date of transference (in case of a professional disease or other damage to health connected with work the previous average wages are preserved until defining a stable loss of the professional ability to work or until the employee's recovery).[135]

If the employee does not agree to do the suggested work, as well as if the appropriate work cannot be suggested, he/she may be dismissed. In this situation the severance pay is obligatory.

133. Article 254 of the RF LC.
134. *See* paras 99–101.
135. Article 182 of the RF LC.

§3. Incapacity to Work Caused by Performance of State or Public Duties

357. An employee is entitled to other rights of keeping his/her place of work, as well as remuneration during the incapacity. For this purpose the concept of guarantees was introduced.[136]

Apart from the general guarantees and compensations stipulated by the RF LC (e.g., working time limitation, annual leave, etc.), special guarantees are provided to employees when performing state or public duties. Under applicable law, if these duties can be performed during working hours, the employees are guaranteed retention of their jobs (employment) and average wages or salaries. The list of such duties is determined by the lawmakers and includes, for example, the exercise of the right to vote; compliance with a summons to appear before agencies of inquiry and investigation, prosecutors and courts as a witness, an expert and translator; participation in court hearings as an assessor, etc. In such instances the employer shall release the employee from the primary work for the period of the performance of the state and public duties.

358. In case of obligation of an employee to carry out regular military service duty (as well as transferring of an employee to an alternative civil service that substitutes military service), the contract of employment has to be terminated in accordance with Article 83 of the RF LC which refers to the grounds which do not depend on the will of the parties.[137]

359. Regarding guarantees for employees chosen to serve on trade unions and committees on labour disagreements, *see* paragraphs 404–406.

§4. Guarantees and Compensation for Employees Combining Work with Study

360. For employees sent for study by an employer, or independently entered into state educational institutions (with state accreditation), and who are successfully studying in the institutions, an employer must provide additional leave with the retention of the average earnings for the established purposes (e.g., taking exams; the preparation of a diploma; and final state examinations). In some instances an employer is obligated to provide non-paid leave.

As concerns employees studying via a correspondence form of study in state-accredited educational institutions of higher professional education, an employer shall pay for travel to and from the place of the location of the relevant educational institution once in an academic year.

---

136. Article 164 of the RF LC.
137. *See also* para. 403, 2(b).

The guarantees and compensation for employees combining work with study in educational institutions lacking state accreditation should be established by a collective agreement, or individual contract of employment.[138]

Special guaranties provided for PhD students have been introduced into the LC in 2014 (Article 173.1).

§5. Incapacity to Work Caused by Other Reasons

361. The RF LC makes reference to other important situations that concern reserving the wage and keeping the place of work for the employees engaged. In particular, employees who are obliged to undergo medical examination in accordance with the RF LC (e.g., employees involved in the sphere of healthcare of public nutrition) are to be paid the average wages for the period of the medical examination.[139]

362. Another example concerns guarantees for employees who are blood donors: the employer is obliged to permit the employee to visit a medical establishment on the day of examination, as well as to pay the established wage. Guarantees for these categories of employees are also referred to in the RF LC. In particular such employees are released from work on the day of giving blood, as well as on the day of medical examination. If the employee came to work on the day of giving blood on the agreement with the employer (except hard work and work with harmful and (or) dangerous labour conditions when the employee's coming to work is impossible), he/she is to be given another day off at his/her request. In case of giving blood and its components during the period of the annual paid leave, on a day off or on a non-working holiday, the employee is to be given another day off at his/her request. After each day of giving blood and its components, the employee is to be given an additional day off. This day off may be added to the annual paid leave at the employee's request or used at other time within the year after the day of giving blood and its components.[140] Here the Law on Giving of Blood and Its Components N125 (last reduction of 7 March 2018) should be also referred to.

363. When the employer sends the employee to improve his/her qualifications with giving up his/her work, the employer reserves the employee's working place (post) and the average wages for the main job. The employees who are sent to improve their qualifications with giving up work to another locality are paid a travelling allowance in accordance with the procedure and in the amounts provided for the employees sent to business trips.[141]

364. In some cases of unlawful dismissal (or transfer of an employee to another job, position), the incapacity to work is caused by the fault of an employer. Workers

---

138. Articles 173–174 of the RF LC. *See also* paras 315 and 324.
139. Article 185 of the RF LC.
140. Article 186 of the RF LC.
141. Article 187 of the RF LC.

involved may have rights to receive payments in accordance with the decisions made by courts.[142]

142. *See* paras 414 and 464.

Chapter 6. Termination of an Individual Contract of Employment

365. Russian LL is based on the principle of closed list of grounds for termination of employment relationship. This means that generally the parties must not formulate any ways of termination of an employment contract besides those prescribed by the legislation. In this respect the LC has the prime interest. It should be taken into account, therewith, that other laws may state additional grounds for termination of an employment contract (*see*, for instance, the RF Law 'On Joint-Stock Companies').[143]

Meanwhile, there are some exceptions from the above principle. For example, according to Article 81 of the LC, an employment contract may be terminated in cases envisaged in the contract with the leader of an enterprise, as well as members of the collective executive body thereof.

§1. Lifetime Employment

366. Employment contracts may be concluded for an indefinite period of time, as well as for a fixed term.[144]

One of the grounds for terminating an employment contract is the end of the duration of a fixed-term contract (Article 79 of the LC). An employment contract concluded for the time of fulfilment of determined work shall be terminated upon the completion of this work. A contract of employment concluded for the time of performance of duties of an absent employee shall be discontinued with the return of this employee to work. A contract concluded for the period of fulfilment of seasonal work is terminated upon the expiry of the determined season.

In the respect of the above, it is important to note that if none of the parties demanded termination of the fixed-term contract upon its expiry, and the employee continues his work after the expiry of the effectivetime period of the contract, the contract is considered to be concluded for an indefinite time. At the same time, an employment contract is concluded for a definite period of time in the absence of sufficient reasons for it is considered to be concluded for indefiniteperiod of time.

367. Regarding some categories of employees, Russian legislation states that they are appointed for their positions until their death (e.g., judges).

§2. General Grounds for Termination of Employment

368. The term 'termination' refers to the ending of employment both at the initiative of an employer and an employee, as well as for other reasons. Termination of employment made by the initiative of an employer is usually called dismissal.

143. The RF Law No. 208-FZ of 26 Dec. 1995, with subsequent amendments and additions.
144. *See* para. 235.

369. Under Russian LL all the methods of termination of a contract of employment may be classified as follows:

(1) termination by mutual agreement of the parties. Both indefinite and fixed-term employment contract may be terminated by mutual consent at any moment (Article 78 of the LC);
(2) termination at the initiative of one party to the contract (by an employer or by an employee) – Articles. 80 and 81 of the RF LC;
(3) termination caused by specific reasons (e.g., the expiry of the contract (Item 2 of Article 58 of the RF LC)), except the cases when the labour relations actually continue and none of the parties has demanded their termination; employee's refusal to continue to work because of change of agreed conditions of the labour contract caused by organizational and technological changes (Article 74 of the LC); employee's refusal to transfer to another job because of health condition as specified in the medical statement (Part 3 of Article 73 of the LC) and some others); and
(4) termination because of circumstances which are not connected to the will of the parties[145] (e.g., the death of an employee or when a candidate was not elected for an appropriate position).

§3. Termination on the Initiative of an Employee

370. Termination of an employment contract on the initiative of an employee should be made in accordance with a certain procedure. Russian LL is based on the principle of freedom of contract; therefore, an employee has the right to terminate an employment contract at any time, usually having warned the employer thereof in written form normally two weeks in advance (Article 80 of the RF LC).

At the same time, it has to be noted that the rule of notification need not be observed in some occasions. In particular, by agreement between the employee and the employer, the contract of employment may be dissolved also before the expiry of the period of warning concerning dismissal. Moreover in cases when the application of an employee regarding dismissal at his initiative (at own wish) stipulated the impossibility to continue the work (e.g., entry into educational institution and retirement), as well as in cases of proved violation by the employer of laws and other normative legal acts containing the norms of LL, as well as conditions of the collective agreement or the employment contract, the employer is obliged to terminate the appropriate contract within the time period specified in the application of the employee.

371. The employee may withdraw his application concerning termination of the contract of employment at any time before the expiry of the period of warning. In this case the termination is not effected. This may occur only if another employee has not been offered this job in writing.

145. Article 83 of the RF LC.

372. Upon the expiry of the agreed period of warning, the employee may stop performing his work. On the last day of work, the employer is obliged to give the labour (work) book to the employee, other documents connected with work, and make final payments. If upon expiry of the period of warning concerning termination of employment, the contract is not dissolved and the employee does not insist on the termination, and this contract is recognized as valid and the operation of it must continue.

373. Previously Russian labour legislation had a restriction on the right to terminate the fixed-term employment contract at the initiative of an employee. According to the Article 32 of the LC of 1971, such employment contracts may be terminated early at the request of an employee in case of his sickness or disability, preventing execution of the contractual work, as well as by other good reasons. Current LC does not contain this requirement.

§4. Termination on the Employer's Initiative

374. The term 'dismissal' usually covers termination of employment at the initiative of an employer. Under Russian LL an employer may dismiss an employee only in situations listed in legislation (with some few exceptions). As a rule an employee has no right to a written statement of the reasons of dismissal.

The majority of reasons for dismissals are specified in the LC (Article 81). These are as follows.

I. Liquidation of an Organization (Enterprise) or Termination of Activities of an Employer, Natural Person

375. The legal notion of liquidation of participants of economic activity is defined by civil legislation. In accordance with Article 61 of CC, a legal person may be liquidated in the following cases:

(1) on the decision of its founders (participants) or others authorized for this purpose by the foundation documents, in the event of expiration of the term for which the legal person was created, as well as an attainment of the purpose for which it was created; declaration by the court of the invalidity of the registration of the legal person in connection with violations of the law or other legal acts which occurred during its creation, if such violations cannot be corrected; and
(2) on the decision of the court, in cases in which the legal person engaged in activities without the required permission (license) or in activities prohibited by law, or violations of the law or actions, which contradict its charter purposes, and some other cases stipulated by legislation.

Liquidation of a legal person entails its termination without transfer of rights and responsibilities in the order of legal succession to other persons. The most important thing for labour relations is that employment contracts are terminated.

376. It should be noted that current LC clarifies the question concerning dismissals at parts of an enterprise. In case of termination of the activity of a branch, representation office or other solitary structural subdivision of organizations located in another territory, dissolution of employment contracts with employees of these structural subdivisions shall be carried out according to the rules envisaged for the cases of liquidation of an organization.

II. Reduction of Staff

377. There is an absolute right of an employer to reduce its personnel. It is only necessary to note that this type of dismissal is connected to complicated procedure, which will be analysed below (*see* paragraphs 389–392).

III. Failure of an Employee to Conform to the Occupied Position for Specified Reasons

378. Regarding the above ground, three reasons might cause the dismissal:

(1) the state of health of an employee proved by medical statement;
(2) insufficient qualification of an employee confirmed by the results of the attestation (certification); and
(3) conflict of interests in cases and under the procedure stipulated by laws (Article 81, Item 7.1 of the LC).

Now the the first reason is no longer applied as a ground for dismissal (in accordance with the recent changes to the RF LC in 2006). The second reason for incapacity to continue the work under the previous conditions requires quite a complicated procedure of attestation that makes this kind of dismissal infrequent. Moreover such dismissals are not legal if employees engaged may not be switched to other work (with their consent).[146]

IV. Change of the Owner of the Property of an Organization

379. The general rule requires that changing of property does not mean termination of contracts with workers automatically. The RF LC contains a special article regulating employment relations in case of a change of owner of a property or an

146. *See* para. 363.

organization, change of jurisdictional subordination of an organization and reorganization thereof. None of these situations is recognized as an independent ground for termination. Employment relationships shall continue with the consent of workers engaged. If the employee refuses to continue to work because of the above changes, the employment contract is discontinued in compliance with Item 6 of Article 77 of the RF LC that reads as a refusal of an employee to continue work in connection with changes of the owner of property of an organization, change of jurisdictional subordination of an organization and reorganization thereof.

But there are some exceptions to the above rule. In particular, in case of a change of owner of property of the organization, the new owner may terminate employment with the manager of the organization, his deputies and the chief accountant no later than within three months from the day of the right of ownership arising.

V. Violations of Labour Discipline

380. The current LC provides the definition of a disciplinary violation (offence) as the failure of performance, or improper performance by a worker through his/her fault of labour duties.

There are two main types of such violations which are recognized as grounds for dismissal. The first one is a repeated failure to perform work by an employee without reasonable grounds. This circumstance may provide to an employer the right to dismiss an employee only if the employee has already received a disciplinary sanction before. Labour legislation (besides the LC) contains the closed list of disciplinary sanctions that may not be changed by contracts of employment. It should be noted that if within a year from the date of application of the disciplinary sanction an employee is not subjected to a new disciplinary sanction, this employee is considered as not to have the above sanction.

The second type of disciplinary violations covers single flagrant violations of labour duties. It is remarkable that legislation contains the closed list of such violations. Primarily they follow from the LC (item 6 of the Article 81). But for certain categories of employees, they are prescribed by other legislative acts.

381. Among so-called single flagrant violations of labour duties listed in the RF LC are the following:

(a) absence from job or at workplace without justifiable reasons for more than four hours in succession of a workday. The place of work should be detailed by employment contracts. If not, court practice refers to the Article 209 of the LC which reads that a workplace is a place where an employee must be situated or where he must arrive in connection with his work and that directly or indirectly is under the control of the employer;
(b) appearing at work in the state of alcoholic, narcotic or other toxic impairment. It has to be mentioned that such dismissal may occur even if an employee appeared in the above conditions somewhere within the territory of an enterprise (organization);

(c) disclosure of a secret protected by law (state, commercial, service, as well as personal data of other workers) which became known to the employee in connection with the performance of labour duties. The appropriate duty of an employee must follow from the contract of employment;
(d) commission at a place of work of stealing of someone's property, other damages of entity proved by judgment of a court which has entered into legal force or decision of the competent body; and
(e) violation by an employee of the requirements for the protection of labour if this violation entailed grave consequences (e.g., accident at work).

382. The procedure of dismissal caused by discipline violation is connected to the established procedure for applying all discipline sanctions by an employer. The main steps of such dismissals are the following:

(1) Before the application of the dismissal, an employer must demand from an employee engaged an explanation in writing. In the event of an employee's refusal to provide it, an appropriate act shall be drawn up. An employee's refusal to provide an explanation shall not be an obstacle to application of a disciplinary sanction (dismissal).
(2) A disciplinary sanction shall be applied not later than one month (for some cases – within six months) from the day of the discovery of the offence, not counting the period of illness, his/her period on vacation, as well as the time necessary to take into account the opinion of the employees' representative body.
(3) Only one disciplinary sanction may be applied for each disciplinary offence.
(4) An employer must issue an order concerning the dismissal which must be announced to the employee within three workdays from the date of publication thereof.

VI. Other Grounds for Dismissal

383. The LC also contains some other reasons for dismissal. For example, an employee may be dismissed in case of submission of forged documents or information known to be false to an employer when concluding the contract.

384. Some grounds for dismissal may be applied only regarding special categories of employees. For example, leaders of enterprises may be dismissed in case of adoption of an unsubstantiated decision which entailed a violation of the preservation of property, unlawful use thereof, or other damage to the property of an organization. For this category of employees, as well as for their deputies, the single flagrant violation is recognized as a ground for their dismissal. Leaders of organizations may be also dismissed in accordance with the grounds prescribed by employment contracts with them.

385. Besides leading personnel there are also other categories of employees who may be dismissed under the terms included into the contract of employment. In particular it concerns employees hired by physical persons[147]and homeworkers.[148] An employee hired by a religious organization may be also dismissed upon the reasons specified in the contract with him/her.[149]

386. Regarding some categories of employees, additional grounds for dismissals are specified in particular chapters of the RF LC. For instance, an employment contract with a person involved in a so-called secondary employment (holding multiple jobs) may be cancelled in the event of the hiring of an employee who will be performing that work as his/her primary job.[150]

387. The LC contains the list of additional reasons for termination of work in a representation of the RF abroad.[151] A contract of employment with such workers may be ceased before the stipulated time also in the following situations:

(1) emergency situation in the country of residence;
(2) declaration of the employee a persona non grata or notification from competent authorities of the country of residence that his (her) residence if it is in this country is unacceptable;
(3) reduction of quota of diplomatic or service personnel of correspondent representations;
(4) non-observance of customs and legislation of a country of residence as well as generally accepted rules of conduct and moral norms by the employee;
(5) failure to execute the obligations under the employment contract by the employee on ensuring observance of legislation in the country of residence, generally accepted rules of conduct and moral norms and rules of residence in force in the representation by members of the employee's family;
(6) temporary disability for the period over two months or in the event of disease preventing to work abroad. The list of such diseases is approved by the RF Government; and
(7) conflict of interests (Article 81, Item 7.1 of the LC) and some others.

388. Not all reasons for dismissal are followed from the RF LC and contracts of employment. Some of them are specified in other federal laws. For example, laws regulating education[152] contain additional grounds for termination of employment with teachers, professors and other employees involved in educational activity. Among such grounds is applying of methods of education which are connected with physical or psychological pressure upon the personality of a student.

147. Article 307 of the RF LC.
148. Article 312 of the RF LC.
149. Article 347 of the RF LC.
150. *See* para. 299.
151. Article 341 of the RF LC.
152. The RF Law 'On Education' of 1996, with amendments; and the RF Law 'On Highest and Postgraduated Professional Education' of 1996, with amendments.

§5. Collective Dismissals

389. Collective dismissals occur in the following situations:

(1) liquidation of an organization (enterprise, other legal persons) or termination of activities by the employer – natural persons;
(2) reduction of the number or personnel establishment of workers (staff).

390. Russian LL provides the scope of guarantees for employees engaged in collective dismissals. In particular it is necessary to realize the following steps of the procedure of collective dismissals.

First, when performing measures to reduce the staff of an organization, an employer should propose to an employee other available work (or a vacant position) corresponding to the employee's skill (qualification) in the same organization. Court practice follows the principle that an employer should suggest to an employee any vacant position which this employee is able to fill (even if it is not in a compliance with his/her qualification).

Second, the employees involved in this dismissal must be warned by an employer personally and over their signature of an impending discharge in connection with the liquidation of an organization and a reduction of the numbers or staff of an organization's employees at least two months before the planned date of dismissal. *See* paragraph 394.

Third, before choosing employees whose positions will be reduced, an employer must take into account the preferential right to remain at work in the event of reduction of staff. This right is defined in Article 179 of LC. First, this right to remain at work shall be granted to employees with a higher labour productivity and qualifications. Second, in the event of equal labour productivity and skill preference in remaining at work shall be given to the following categories of employees:

(1) persons with family responsibilities – when they have two or more dependents and other legally specified members;
(2) employees whose family lacks other workers with independent earnings;
(3) employees who received accident at work with a severe labour injury or occupational illness in the given organization;
(4) some categories of disabled persons; and
(5) employees who raised their skill in the employer's area without interruption of work.

Finally, other categories of an organization's employees enjoying a preferential right to remain at work may be prescribed by a collective agreement.

391. Russian LL has a special term 'mass dismissals' which may be determined in accordance with the criteria provided by legislation. In case of the threat of such mass dismissals, an employer, taking into account the opinion of the elected trade union body, shall take necessary steps stipulated by legislation, appropriate collective agreements and individual employment contracts.

392. Regarding the procedure of collective dismissals, it is necessary to note that the dismissals of members of trade unions may be realized only with the consent of the appropriate trade union.

§6. TERMS OF NOTICE

393. Concerning termination of all types of employment contracts at the employee's initiative, there is a general rule that an employee has a right to terminate an employment contract at any moment, having warned the employer thereof in written form two weeks in advance (Article 80 of the RF LC).

394. Regarding the terms of notification, it is necessary to mention collective dismissals.[153] In case of liquidation of an organization, as well as reduction of staff, the employees involved must be warned by an employer personally and over their signature not less than two months before the date of the dismissal. This period may be reduced in accordance with the written agreement between the employer and the employee. In this case the employer has the right to dissolve the employment contract with this particular employee without warning of two months in advance with the simultaneous payment of additional contributory compensation in the amount of the two months average earnings.

395. Labour legislation also establishes some specific requirements as regards notification. Mostly they are referred to certain categories of employees. For example, an employee who has entered into an employment contract for a period of less than two months is required to give his/her employer three calendar days' written notice about the earlier termination of the contract. An employer who has hired such a temporary worker is obliged to provide to a worker the written notice (with return receipt) about the termination of employment due to the organization's liquidation or stuff reduction not less than three calendar days before the date of this dismissal.

Seasonal workers[154] are required to notify the employer three days before termination of the contract in a written form. At the same time, in case of liquidation of an organization the employer should notify a seasonal employee seven calendar days before the dismissal (shorter period as compared to a general procedure of collective dismissals).[155]

The leader of an organization is entitled to terminate a labour contract early (before the date of its expiry), giving written notice to the employer (owner of the organization's property or latter's representative) no later than one month in advance.[156]

153. *See* paras 396–399.
154. *See* para. 222.
155. Article 296 of the RF LC.
156. Article 280 of the RF LC.

§7. Severance Pay

396. Severance pay is a special payment provided at the end of an employment relationship by an employer. The legal claim on severance payments depends on reasons of termination of employment and is not connected to the period (years) of employment.

The Russian LC establishes severance allowances in the following situations:

(1) In the case of liquidation of an organization (Article 81, Item 1 of the RF LC) or a reduction of a staff of an organization (Article 81, Item 2 of the RF LC), an employee engaged shall be paid a severance allowance in the amount of the average monthly earnings. Additionally he/she will retain the average monthly earnings for a period of job placement but not more than two months from the day of the discharge (taking into account the severance allowance). In exceptional cases the average monthly earnings will, by a decision of a public employment service agency, be retained by an employee for three months from the day of a discharge, provided that the employee had applied to that agency within a two-week period of the discharge and had not been placed in a job by it.

(2) A severance allowance to the amount of the two-week average wage has to be in connection with the following situations:
   (a) employee's refusal to change an occupied position or performed work due to a state of health that prevents continuation of the given work;
   (b) assignment of the employee to military service (or alternative civil service substituting for it);[157]
   (c) the restoration to work of an employee who previously performed the work;
   (d) an employee's refusal of a transfer in connection with the relocation of the employer to another territorial division; and
   (e) when an employee is recognized to be totally unable to perform any labour activity in accordance with medical document and so on.

397. Severance pay is specifically defined for some categories of employees. For example, in the event of termination of an employment contract with the leader of an organization (director), deputies thereof, and chief bookkeeper in connection with a change of owner of the organization, the new owner is obliged to pay contributory compensation to the above employees in an amount of not less than three average monthly wages of the employee.

When a contract of employment with a seasonal worker is terminated due to the organization's liquidation, severance pay shall be made in the amount of two-week average wage of the employee engaged.[158]

398. Regarding employment with an individual employer (a physical person), the period of the notice to be given upon termination, as well as the cases when the

157. *See also* para. 365.
158. Article 296 of the RF LC.

severance pay and other compensation must be paid upon cancellation of an employment contract, shall be determined in the employment contract.[159]

399. Contracts of employment, as well as collective agreements, may stipulate other cases of the payment of severance allowances and their higher amounts (Article 178 of thr LC). This rule is not applied to cases of disciplinary dismissals.

§8. Immediate Dismissal

400. Immediate dismissal may occur in case of termination of a contract of employment with leaders of organizations. In particular, in case of a change of owner of property of the organization, the new owner may terminate employment with the manager of the organization, his/her deputies and the chief accountant no later than within three months from the day of the right of ownership arising.

A contract of employment with the leader of an organization may be terminated before the date of its expiry in other situations too. The termination shall be based on the decision of an authorized body of the organization, the owner or the person (the institution) authorized by the owner. The authorized body is not obliged to explain why the leader was dismissed. But in case of such a dismissal in the absence of guilty actions (inaction) of the leader, he/she shall be paid compensation for early termination of the labour contract. The amount of the compensation must be defined by the employment contract and should not be less than three salaries of the employee engaged.[160]

§9. Protection of Certain Employees in the Sphere of Dismissals

I. Young Workers

401. Termination of employment at the employer's initiative (except cases where an organization is liquidated) with employees under 18 years of age may be recognized as lawful only with the permission of the corresponding state labour inspectorate and the commission for children and the protection of their rights (Article 269 of the LC).

II. Women

402. It is very important to mention that labour legislation prohibits dismissals of pregnant women on the employer's initiative (except for cases of liquidation of the organization or termination of activities of the employer out of natural persons).

159. Article 307 of the RF LC.
160. Article 279 of the RF LC.

Women who have children under 3 years of age, as well as single mothers raising a children under 14 years of age (or a disabled child under 18 years of age), may be dismissed only in case of their disciplinary violations.

III. Disabled

403. As already mentioned above, invalidity itself does not automatically cause termination of employment with the appropriate person. The termination may be doneonly while observing an established procedure.[161]

§10. Protection of Employees Involved in Representing Workers' Rights

I. Workers Who Belong to Collective Elective Trade Union Bodies and Have Not Been Released from Their Primary Job

404. In some cases the termination of employment at the employer's initiative with the workers above is allowed, aside from general termination procedures, only upon the consent of the corresponding superior elective trade union body.[162] In particular this concerns staff reduction; insufficient qualification and some other cases.

II. Workers Elected to Trade Union Bodies and Released from Their Jobs

405. Upon the expiration of his/her term of office at trade union organization, the employee who was released from the job due to the election shall be offered his/her former job (position) or, in the absence of the latter and with the worker's consent, another equivalent job (position) in the same organization. Only if the employee rejects the job (position) offered him/her may the employment contract be terminated.[163]

III. Workers Involved in the Procedures for Settlement of Collective Industrial Disputes

406. Members of the Commission for Conciliation, industrial arbitrators, while considering collective industrial dispute, shall be relieved from their principal employment with their average wage being reserved, for a period of not more than three months in one year. Representatives of employees, who participate in a settlement of collective industrial dispute, may not be, for the period of such settlement,

161. *See* para. 363.
162. Article 374 of the RF LC.
163. Article 375 of the RF LC.

subject to any disciplinary punishment, re-engaged or dismissed upon the employer's initiative without prior consent of the authorizing body.[164]

§11. Reinstatement

407. The decision on reinstatement of employee, who was dismissed unlawfully, is made by the court, as well as by the State Labour Inspection. The employee shall be re-engaged in his/her previous job, and this decision is the subject to immediate enforcement. In case of delay of enforcement of such a decision by an employer, the respective body must determine a payment to the employee of the average wage (or the wage difference) for the whole period of the delay.[165]

164. Article 405 of the RF LC.
165. Article 396 of the RF LC.

Chapter 7. Protection of Certain Categories of Workers and Protection Against Discrimination in Employment

408. The legal rules on protection of certain categories of employees (vulnerable groups) are based on general principles of prohibition of discrimination, as well as on differentiation in regulation of labour.

The RF LC as well as other legal acts detail the above principles. For instance, the RF Law 'On Employment'[166] also envisages additional guarantees for the following groups starting work: young people, single parents, disabled and individuals approaching retirement. Furthermore, non-discrimination in the workplace for separate categories of workers is regulated by collective agreements, as well as individual contracts of employment.[167]

§1. Female Workers, Young Workers, Employees with Family Responsibilities and the Disabled

I. Female Employees

409. The RF Constitution states that motherhood and childhood, as well as the family, are under state protection.[168] Russian LL provides some particulars in the sphere of regulation of work undertaken by female employees. There is a special chapter of the LC which is devoted to the rights of employed women.

410. On the whole, Russian legislation guarantees the special protection of female employees.

First, the limitations on hiring female employees to some jobs are established. In particular the use of female labour is forbidden in jobs involving manual lifting and moving of heavy objects in excess of the allowable limits for women.[169]

The use of female labour should be limited in heavy labour and jobs involving harmful and/or dangerous work conditions, and also in underground jobs, with the exception of non-physical labour and jobs in the area of sanitary/medical and consumer services.[170]

411. Regarding guarantees connected to maternity, it is necessary to mention the following:

---

166. The RF Law No. 1032-1 of 19 Apr. 1991 'On Employment of the Population of the Russian Federation' (redrafted Federal Law No. 36-FZ of 20 Apr. 1996, with subsequent additions and amendments).
167. *See also* paras 251 and 328.
168. Article 38 of the RF Constitution.
169. Article 253 of the RF LC.
170. *See* 'The List of Heavy Works Involving Harmful and/or Dangerous Work Conditions, Where the Use of Female Labour Is Banned' approved by The Decision of the Government of the RF No. 162 of 25 Feb. 2000. *See also* paras 293, 300 and 304.

(1) It is not allowed to recruit for working in shifts pregnant females and females with children under 3 years of age.[171] It is prohibited to send pregnant women on business trips, as well as to assign them to work overtime or at night, on weekends or on non-working holidays.
(2) It is also prohibited to refuse to hire women for reasons connected with pregnancy or the existence of children. Such a refusal may be appealed in a court of law.
(3) There are restrictions on employers as concerns hiring, changing and terminating of employment with pregnant women (e.g., upon a pregnant woman's request and pursuant to a medical finding, standards of output and service shall be reduced or she shall be transferred to another job; it is prohibited to dismiss a pregnant woman at the initiative of an employer, with the exception of cases where an organization is liquidated).[172]
(4) Female employees must be granted maternity leave (at their request and pursuant to a medical finding, women are to be granted maternity leave of the period of time calculated in accordance with LC). According to Article 255 of the LC, women workers are granted 70 calendar days pre-natal leave (in the event of the birth of two or more children – 84 calendar days) and 70 calendar days post-natal leave (or in the event of a complicated delivery – 86 and in the event of the birth of two or more children – 110 calendar days).

The leave for taking care of a child (until the age of 3 years) may be used in full or in part, with the right of the employees to keep their position.

II. Employees with Family Responsibilities

412. Russian legislation provides additional guarantees for persons with family responsibilities. Usually this concerns persons who are taking care of children or other dependants. For instance, the leave for the purposes of child caring may be granted in full or partially to the child's father, grandmother, grandfather, other relatives or tutor actually nursing him (her).

413. Some guarantees are connected to taking care of a disabled child. For instance, upon the written request of one parent (a tutor) he (she) may be granted four additional paid free days per month for nursing handicapped children and persons handicapped from birth up to 18 years of age. These days may be used by one of the above-mentioned persons or divided among them in their discretion.[173]

Single parents as well as carers of non-adultsare granted the guarantees and privileges given to females in connection with their maternity (reduction of night works, etc.; and additional leave).

171. Article 298 of the RF LC.
172. *See also* para. 409.
173. Article 262 of the RF LC.

414. A collective agreement may provide additional annual non-paid leave up to 14 calendar days for an employee with two or more children at the age under 14 years, the employee with a handicapped child under 18 years of age, the single female parent nursing a child under 14 years of age and the single male parent nursing a child under 14 years of age at any time convenient to them.[174]

III. Young Workers

415. Russian LL establishes the minimum age for employment as 16. In some cases, which are strictly stipulated by the LC, it is allowed to employ younger workers.[175]

416. Mostly additional guarantees in the sphere of labour cover workers under 18 years of age. The level of the guaranties differs depending on definite age of a particular employee, on types of work and some other characteristics (for instance, whether an employee combines the work with studying).

417. First, work of persons under 18 years of age in hazardous or dangerous conditions, in the underground, as well as at jobs that harm their moral development and health (gambling business, cabarets and night clubs, in production cycles, transportation and sale of alcoholic beverages, tobacco goods, narcotic and toxic compounds) is prohibited. It is also banned for minors to carry or move workloads in excess of the limits set for them.

418. Second, persons under the age of 18 may be hired only after an obligatory preliminary medical examination, and shall be subject to obligatory medical examinations annually until reaching the age of 18.[176] For such categories of young employees, reduced labour norms may be introduced (Article 270 of the LC).

Regarding the termination of contracts of employment, *see* paragraph 401.

419. Third, wages shall be paid to workers under the age of 18 by taking into account their reduced work hours. An employer may offer them additional payments at his/her own expense, up to the level of the pay scale for full-time workers of the corresponding categories.

Compensation for the labour of workers under 18 years of age who are students in general education institutions and institutions of basic, secondary and higher vocational education and work during time free from their studies shall be made in proportion to time worked or based on their output. An employer may establish payments to such workers in addition to their wages, at his/her own expense.[177]

---

174. Article 263 of the RF LC.
175. *See also* paras 242 and 243.
176. Article 266 of the RF LC.
177. Article 271 of the RF LC.

420. It is prohibited to send workers under 18 years of age on business trips, to engage them in overtime work, night work and during holidays.[178]

421. Workers under the age of 18 years are entitled to a longer annual paid leave of 31 calendar days.[179]

422. The RF LC no longer has the provision on prescribed allocation (so-called official distribution of young specialists) jobs for youth employment, which, in particular, have given rise to additional problems with employment of young persons. Legislation on employment establishes some possibilities in the sphere of promotion of employment as concerns such persons. In particular, legislation states that job quotas for juveniles must be observed.

Since 1995 the contractual system of employment promotion of young specialists has been applied. Moreover, educational institutions may conclude contracts on forthcoming hiring of their students with both students and employers interested. Under such contracts the young specialist is obliged to conclude a fixed-term contract of employment with the employer suggested by the educational institution.

423. In accordance with the legislation on education, the state guarantees universal access to free non-specialized education at primary, basic and intermediate (complete) levels. Beyond this, professional education at intermediate, higher and postgraduate levels is available – but only on a competitive entry basis in national and local educational establishments, and only if it is for the first time. Taking into account the requirements and potential of the student, teaching can take place face-to-face in daytime classes, or in evening classes or through distance learning. It can also take the form of family education, self-education or courses away from home.

Employees who combine work with study have some additional guarantees in the sphere of employment.[180]

IV. Disabled

424. According to the legislation on education,[181] as well as to the RF laws 'On Social Protection of Disabled People in the Russian Federation' (Article 19); and 'On Employment of the Population of the Russian Federation' (Article 13), disabled people are given the right to receive free professional education; to receive preferential access to educational institutions; to receive state grants throughout their courses; and to use sign language interpretation.

---

178. Article 268 of the RF LC.
179. Article 267 of the RF LC.
180. *See also* paras 365 and 367.
181. The RF Law No. 12-FZ 'On Education' of 13 Jan. 1996, with subsequent additions and amendments.

Their status in employment is also connected to certain additional guarantees. Regarding termination of employment with disabled workers,[182] disabled people enjoy specific guarantees in the sphere of employment promotion by the RF legislation.[183]

§2. Measures to Promote Equal Treatment

I. Constitutional Provisions

425. In compliance with the RF Constitution, all people are equal before the law and court (Article 19, Part 1).

The RF Constitution also guarantees the equality of rights and freedoms for all citizens, regardless of sex, race, nationality, language, origin, property and official status, place of residence, religion, convictions, membership of public associations and also of other circumstances. All forms of limitations of human rights on social, racial, national, linguistic or religious grounds are banned (Article 19, Part 2).

Part 2 of Article 17 of the Constitution stipulates that fundamental human rights and freedoms are inalienable and to be enjoyed by everyone from the day of birth, while Part 3 of Article 55 determines that the rights and freedoms of man and citizen may be limited by the federal law only to such an extent to which it is necessary for the protection of the fundamental principles of the constitutional system, morality, health, the rights and lawful interests of other people, for ensuring defence of the country and security of the state.

II. Labour Law

426. The RF LC (Article 3) includes provisions prohibiting discrimination. In particular it states that everyone has equal opportunities to implement labour rights; no one may be a subject to restrictions on labour rights and liberties or obtain any advantages regardless of sex, race, colour of the skin, nationality, language, origin, property, family or social status and occupational position, age, place of residence, attitude to religion, political views, affiliation or failure to affiliate with public associations, as well as other circumstances not pertaining to the business properties of the employee. The establishment of distinctions, exceptions, preferences, as well as restrictions of rights of employees which are determined by specific requirements of a particular type of work that are specified in a federal law, or stipulated by a care of the state concerning persons needing heightened social and legal protection, are not recognized as discrimination (such as preferences for pregnant women and disabled persons).

In spite that Russian legislation in general does not offer effective remedies against discrimination and compensation for incurred damage, the LC stipulates that persons who believe that they were subject to discrimination in the sphere of labour

182. *See* para. 363.
183. *See* paras 435–438.

shall be entitled to apply to the court with a claim to restore their violated rights, reimbursing incurred damage and compensating for moral harm. At the same time, there are practically no rules countering discrimination directly or aimed at establishing mechanisms to eradicate discriminating practices and restore violated rights. In the sphere of labour, mostly people are subject to discriminatory treatment on the grounds of the absence of registration at the place of residence.

427. Disputes on discrimination in the sphere of hiring can be appealed directly to the courts. If the court decides the allegations have been proved, it will rule that the discrimination be stopped, compensation be awarded to the victim for material and moral damages and the employer be required to hire the complainant. Officials found guilty of discrimination, particularly in their hiring policy, will be held to account (and even criminally responsible). Thus violations of equal rights – on grounds of gender, race, nationality, language, origins, wealth and social status, place of residence, attitude to religion, beliefs and membership of a non-governmental organization – that infringe the rights and lawful interests of citizens will, depending on their gravity, be punished in accordance with criminal law (Article 136 of the RF Criminal Code).[184]

§3. Guarantees in the Sphere of Promotion of Employment

428. Federal legislation prescribes the obligation of employers to create jobs for some categories of vulnerable groups of employees (e.g., disabled) in accordance with obligatory quotas. Whereas the former LC included the rule on the employers' obligation to create workplaces (in accordance with established quotas) for these categories of persons, the current LC contains only a reference regarding specific features of employment of a certain categories of employees (e.g., young workers, women and disabled).[185]

429. Actually the obligation to employ within the established quotas is prescribed by the federal legislation only with respect to the disabled. One of the priorities of state employment policy is to assist the disabled in finding work. In accordance with existing legislation, the following integrated services are provided to the disabled who have applied for help in finding work:

- consultations for professional guidance;
- assistance in looking for work;
- professional training;
- allocation to posts by quota; and
- assistance in setting up small businesses and working as a self-employed person,

In accordance with the RF Law 'On Social Protection of the Disabled in the RF', employers having an average definite number of employees are obliged to create

184. The RF Criminal Code, adopted by the RF Law of 13 Jun. 1996 No. 63-FZ, with subsequent amendments and additions.
185. Article 272 of the RF LC.

jobs for the disabled within definite quotas. Other organizations, including public associations of the disabled and organizations set up by them, companies and communities in which the authorized capital stock consists of contributions made by the public association of the disabled, are excluded from the obligation to create jobs for disabled. Usually the quotas are defined at the level of subjects of the RF (e.g., in Moscow legislation).

430. Enterprises – regardless of the legal and organizational structure, as well as the property base – are obliged to donate wages for each disabled person within their quota. Many companies, however, lack the conditions for employing disabled people. In case of impossibility to observe the fixed quota for employment of the disabled, employers have to make obligatory monthly payments to the budgets of the subjects of the RF for every unemployed disabled person within the limits of the fixed quota. The limitations and procedures for making these payments are specified at the level of the subjects of the RF. The amount of payment for each unemployed disabled person is equal to the minimum living wage for the able-bodied population approved in the RF by the date of payment.

431. Subjects of the RF may detail the above requirements at the appropriate legal acts. In particular the Law of Moscow 'On Quotation of Workplaces in Moscow' (adopted in 2004, applied with following amendments) prescribes that the above quota comprises 4% of the personnel in organizations with more than 100 employees (the maximum permitted by the federal legislator). Employment of the disabled by the employer, confirmed by conclusion of employment contracts with them according to which the period of work in the current month was not less than fifteen calendar days, is regarded as satisfactory fulfilment of this quota.

Chapter 8. Covenants of Non-competition and Inventions by Employees

§1. Covenants of Non-competition

432. There is a general rule that Russian LL does not contain limitations in the sphere of possible competition of an employee with his/her employer.

But the situation of competition may occur in case of the employee performing several jobs under several contracts of employment with different employers. According to the RF LC, the rules regulating holding of multiple jobs (that understood as performance of another regular paid job, under an employment contract, outside of the time of performing the main job, also is called as secondary employment) do not provide any restrictions regarding non-competition. Mainly this approach is based on the principle that an employee as being involved in subordinate employment relationship with every employer may not compete with the employer.[186]

Some exceptions from the above rule exist. Mainly they concern certain categories of employees. Particularities of performing of secondary jobs are defined for employees involved in the educational, medical, pharmaceutical spheres, etc.

433. Some restrictions in connection with the above also apply to leaders of organizations. They follow from the RF LC, as well as from the legislation establishing the legal status of enterprises (legal persons). In particular the LC states that the head of an organization has the right to hold paid posts in other organizations only upon an agreement of the organization-authorized body, property owner or authorized agent (body) of the owner. The organization head has no right to participate in inspection and control bodies of this organization.[187]

434. It should be noted that subcontracting as another form of secondary employment may be performed under conditions of civil law contracts. To the workers engaged in civil law relationships, civil law is applied. In this respect the rules stated by the legislation on non-competition are applied.

435. Non-competition may be also guaranteed by including into contracts of employment the clauses on the observing of commercial secrecy. Some contracts of employment contain a requirement not to disclosure commercial secrecy during a definite period upon the termination of a contract. The legislation on commercial secrecy provides such a possibility. In particular the RF Law No. 98-FZ of 29 July 2004 'On Commercial Secrecy' (with following changes) states the period of time during which the person is obliged to keep the commercial secrecy received during employment. This period is counted as three years from the date of termination of the appropriate contract of employment.

186. *See also* paras 299–301.
187. Article 276 of the RF LC. *See also* para. 219.

§2. Inventions by Employees

436. Matters related to employees' inventions are governed by the RF civil legislation, in particular by legislation on patents and copyright law. Currently the CC (Part IV) is applied in this respect, as well as instructions regarding filing and processing patent applications which are issued by the State Patent Authority.

Some guarantees for inventors are stated by the legislation of the USSR. In particular the USSR Law of 31 May 1991 'On Inventions of the USSR' is still applied where it does not contradict the current Russian legislation.

Russia has acceded to the Patent Cooperation Treaty and the International Convention for the Protection of Industrial Property as revised in Stockholm (Paris Convention 1883). Russia is also a member of Eurasian patent convention, which was concluded between CIS countries and provides for a single 'Eurasian patent' effective in member countries.

437. In accordance with the legislation on patents, an employer may require the rights for employees' inventions if they were created in the course of duty obligations or in the performance of an assignment expressly given by the employer (service-related work). It is important to note that the creation of a new model, technology, etc., may be recognized as an invention if it was done during employment relationships. Otherwise an employer may not receive any right to it.

438. Usually rights to an invention developed by an employee belong to the employer, unless otherwise provided by a contract of employment. However, the employee has the right to mention his/her name or demand such mention in connection with any exploitation of the invention. Therefore an individual contract of employment plays a significant role in the sphere of employees' inventions.

The inventor also has the right to receive remuneration. The amount of the remuneration of the author for each form of use of the service-related work, and the manner of the payment thereof, shall be specified in the contract concluded by the author and employer.

For the purposes of avoiding possible conflicts, it is strongly recommended to clarify the questions above in individual contracts of employment. For instance, legislation on patents does not define the exact amount of remuneration for an invention. This topic has to be clarified by the agreement of the parties of an employment relationship.

439. An employer has an option to obtain patents to inventions, utility models and industrial designs which were developed by employees in its name. If the employer does not file a patent application within four months after notification by the author about development of an invention, the author has the right to file a patent application and obtain patent for his/her name.

Patents for inventions are effective for a definite period of time from the date of filing the application. Patents for utility models are effective for an initial term of five years which may be extended by three years. Industrial designs are protected for an initial period of ten years which may be extended by five years.

Patent owners have exclusive rights to manufacture, use, import, offer for sale, sell or otherwise put into circulation or store with these purpose products containing the patented invention, utility model or industrial design, or products manufactured using the method protected by the patent. Exclusive or non-exclusive right to use a patent may be assigned or granted by the owner to another party.

440. Registration of patent assignment and licence agreements with the national patent authority are required. Unregistered agreements are deemed void. The 'Rules for Registration of Agreements on Transfer of the Exclusive Rights in Invention, Utility Model, Industrial Design, Trademark, Service mark, Registered Layouts of Integrated Microcircuits or the Right to Use Them, and on Transfer of Exclusive Rights in Software or Database in Full or Partially' are endorsed by the Russian Agency for Patents and Trademarks.

441. An employer has exceptional rights to the results of the creative works (scientific, literature, etc.) of employees, if another rule is not defined by the contract of employment. The use of such works begins not later than three years since their producing (Article 1295 of the RF CC).

The above provisions are not applied to the making of encyclopaedias, encyclopaedic dictionaries, collections of scientific works published in one or in several periodical publications, even if the work was done in the course of duty obligations or the performance of an assignment expressly given by the employer.

Chapter 9. Settlement of Individual Labour Disputes

442. The RF Constitution recognizes the right to individual and collective labour disputes with the use of means of resolution thereof established by federal laws, including the right to strike.[188] The LL of the RF provides for different settlement procedures depending on whether the dispute is the individual or the collective one.

§1. The Notion of an Individual Labour Dispute

443. Article 381 of the RF LC defines an individual labour dispute as a disagreement between a worker and an employer concerning the application of labour legislation and other legal normative acts, collective agreements, as well as conditions of the contract of employment.

A dispute between an employer and a person who was in employment relations with the said employer earlier, as well as a person wishing to enter into an employment contract in case the employer refuses to enter such a contract, is considered an individual labour dispute.

444. Individual labour disputes are widespread in Russia. For example, in 2003 LL cases were estimated as 12.8% of all civil law cases. Among them 81% was caused by violations of employers in the sphere of paying of wages; 5.2% concerned dismissals; and 1.6% were about accidents at work.[189]

Quite often an employer tries to avoid entering into labour relations and replaces an employment contract by a civil law contract. This deprives the worker of many rights envisaged by the labour legislation. This practice also provides a lot of reasons for individual labour disputes.

445. As regards the procedures on individual labour disputes settlement, it is possible to define three main categories of disputes:

(1) a general scheme envisaging a sequential examination of a dispute in the Commission on Individual Labour Disputes (hereinafter 'the LDC') and in the court. A dispute can be resolved in the commission if its decision is not appealed against by the parties (by a party) and brought to the court;
(2) a judicial scheme where examination of the dispute begins directly in the court avoiding the LDC; and
(3) a special scheme where some categories of disputes are examined in accordance with specific norms of procedure.

446. It is necessary to add that previously trade unions had the right to settle labour disputes. Current legislation provides trade unions only with the right to participate in settlement of collective labour disputes. In particular Article 14 of the RF

188. Article 37 of the RF Constitution.
189. *Rossiiskaya Gazeta*, 21 Nov. 2003. *See* www.rg.ru.

Law defining the status of trade unions makes reference to their right only to participate in settling collective labour disputes, as well as to organize, in conformity with federal legislation (laws), strikes, meetings, demonstrations, picketing and other industrial actions, making use thereof as a means for protection of the social and labour rights and interests of employees.

§2. Settlement of Individual Labour Disputes by the Labour Dispute Commission

447. Labour dispute commissions are formed on the initiative of employees and (or) employer from the representatives of employees and employer in equal numbers. Representatives of employees are elected to the LDC by the general meeting (conference) of employees of an organization or are delegated by the representative body of employees with subsequent approval by the generalmeeting (conference) of employees of an organization. Representatives of an employer are appointed to the commission by the head of an organization.

The LDC may be formed at enterprises, as well as in their structural divisions.

448. An employee can submit an appeal to the LDC within the period of three months, since the moment he/she learned or was supposed to learn about the infringement of his/her right. If the period set is missed for valid reasons, the LDC can restore the period and solve the dispute in essence.

449. The main aspects of the procedure of the settlement of a dispute by the LDC are followed from the LC RF. The particulars of the procedure may be stated in collective agreements, as well as in other local acts of the organizations (e.g., Regulations on the LDC).

The labour dispute shall be considered by the LDC within ten calendar days from the date of the receipt of the worker's application. Consideration of a dispute in the absence of the worker is permitted only upon his/her written consent.

The LDC has the right to summon witnesses and invite experts. On demand of the commission, the head of an organization must provide the commission with all necessary documents in the period set.

A decision is taken by the LDC by a simple majority of its members participating in the consideration of the dispute.[190]

450. If the LDC has not considered the dispute within ten days, the worker has the right to withdraw his/her appeal and submit the case before a court of law. If the LDC has considered the dispute but the worker disagrees with the decision, he or she can submit the case before a court of law within ten days.[191]

190. Articles 387 and 388 of the RF LC.
191. Article 390 of the RF LC.

451. The decision of the LDC is subject to enforcement within three days upon expiry of ten days period provided for appeal. In case of failure to enforce the decision in the established period of time, the LDC shall issue to employee a special certificate. On the basis of this certificate, the officer of the court (who is responsible for execution of courts' decisions) realizes the compulsory execution of the decision.[192]

§3. The Role of Courts

452. As has already been mentioned, there are no specialized labour courts in the RF. Labour disputes are handled by the courts of general jurisdiction (*see* paragraphs 20, 21 and 23).

However, the question of establishingof special courts as one of the elements of reforming of judicial system is being widely discussed.

453. The Constitution of the RF (Article 118) does not foresee independent judicial labour proceedings. At present, individual labour disputes are handled by the above courts in accordance with the civil courts' procedure established by the RF Civil Procedural Code.[193]

454. According to the general rule, courts consider individual labour disputes upon claims sent by employees, employers or trade unions, if the mentioned subjects disagree with the decision of the LDC.

In some cases an individual labour dispute is submitted directly (without its consideration by the LDC) to a court. These cases as stipulated by the RF LC include, *inter alia*, the following situations:

(a) when a worker asks to be reinstated in his/her position, regardless of the basis for terminating his/her labour contract; to change the date or the wording of reasons given for the termination; to be transferred to another job; to be reimbursed for time missed due to a forced absence; or for a difference in wages during a period when he/she performed lower-paid work;
(b) upon the request of an employer for restitution by a worker of damages caused to the organization, unless otherwise stipulated by federal laws;
(c) disputes concerning a hiring rejection;
(d) disputes of persons working under employment contracts concluded with individual employers; and
(e) disputes of persons who believe they were subject to discrimination.

455. An individual labour dispute can be submitted to the court within a three-month period. In case of termination of employment at the employer's initiative, the

192. Article 389 of the RF LC.
193. Enforced by the RF Law of 14 Nov. 2002 No. 138-FZ, applied with subsequent amendments and additions.

mentioned period is stated as one month. The employer can appeal for compensation of damages inflicted by the worker within a one-year period. She/he can appeal for non-paid salary within one-year period too. [194]

If the above-mentioned periods are missed with good cause, they may be extended by a court.

456. According to Article 393 of the LC, employees are relieved from paying court expenses. This rule is also applied in cases of recognition of civil law contracts for work and services to be employment ones.

457. If the court considering an individual labour dispute finds the dismissal, as well as the transfer of the worker, to be unjustified, the worker is reinstated by the court. The court examining the individual labour dispute issues a judgment ordering that the employee be paid his/her average wage for the entire period of forced absence at work (caused by unlawful dismissal). In case of transfer to another job, the difference in wages for the entire period during which he/she performed lower-paid work must be compensated.

The court also may change the ground for termination of a contract of employment. In particular if the reasons given for a termination are declared incorrect, or do not conform to law, the court examining the individual labour dispute is required to indicate in its ruling the reason and basis for the termination in strict conformity with the wording of the RF LC or other federal law. If an incorrect wording of reasons given for a termination in the workbook of the employee has prevented the employee from beginning another job, a court shall issue a judgment regarding paying his/her average wage for the entire period of forced absence from work.[195]

In the above situations, the court may at the worker's request issue a judgment that the worker be compensated monetarily for psychological damage caused him/her by the indicated actions. The amount of such compensation shall be determined by the court.

194. Article 392 of the RF LC.
195. Article 394 of the RF LC.

Part II. Collective Labour Relations

Chapter 1. Trade Union Freedom

458. Trade unions are voluntary organizations that unite working people for the purpose of defending the social and economic rights and interests of their members. The legal status of Russian trade unions is defined in the RF Constitution, as well as the RF LC. The legal status of trade unions in Russia is also defined by the RF Law No. 10-FZ 'On Trade Unions, Their Rights and Guarantees for Performance of Their Activities' of 12 January 1996, applied with subsequent amendments. The most recent of them are enforced from 1 January 2017 (hereinafter – The Law on Trade Unions) which is applicable to the extent that it is not contradicted by current LC.

459. The rights of trade unions are also guaranteed by international legal acts, including ratified ILO conventions (e.g., Convention 84 concerning the Right of Association and the Settlement of Labour Disputes in Non-metropolitan Territories, 1947; and Convention 87 on Freedom of Association and Protection of the Right to Organize, 1948).

The RF legislation on trade unions, their establishment and rights, is generally consistent with the international standards of freedom of association. Problems arise in the application of this legislation, including a lack of mechanisms for realization of many provisions such as, for example, provisions on prohibiting discrimination for involvement in trade union activities or interference with such activities.

§1. Freedom to Establish and Join Trade Unions

460. Article 30 of the RF Constitution prescribes that everyone shall have the right to association, including the right to create trade unions in order to protect one's interests.

The ILO Convention 87 on Freedom of Association and Protection of the Right to Organize, 1948 confirms the above right. In particular Article 2 of this Convention states that workers and employers, without distinction whatsoever, have the right to establish and, subject only to the rules of the organization concerned, to join organizations of their own choosing without previous authorization.

461. According to the Article 2 of the RF Law on Trade Unions, a trade union is a voluntary public entity of workers linked by common professional interests, according to the type of their activity, set up for the purposes of representation and protection of their social labour rights and interests. All trade unions enjoy equal rights.

Every person of 14 years of age and above engaged in labour (professional) activities has the right to set up, at his/her discretion, trade unions for the protection of his/her interests, as well as to join these, and to engage in trade union activity.

Foreign citizens and stateless persons who are residents in RF territory may be members of Russian trade unions, except in the cases established by federal laws or international treaties with participation of the RF.

462. The legislation does not impose any restrictions of the right to establish federations and confederations, to join international federations and confederations. But quite often in reality, registering agencies insist that only trade unions registered as legal entities are entitled to establish a trade union association (Federation), referring to general provisions of civil law regulating the establishment and registration of legal entities, including associations of legal entities. In compliance with the CC, a union (association) is a type of a legal entity with a membership of constituent legal entities. Therefore, justice departments believe that trade unions operating without legal entity status may not join in, or register their association.

§2. Freedom of Trade Union Activity

463. The RF Law on Trade Unions states that these organizations are independent in their activity from the organs of executive power, the organs of local self-government, employers and their amalgamations (unions, associations), political parties and other public entities, and shall not be accountable to them or subject to their control. Any interference by state bodies, bodies of local self-government and their officials in the activity of trade unions, which may entail a restriction of trade union rights or hinder the legitimate exercise of their activity, is prohibited (Article 5 of the above law). This rule is developing international standards, in particular, the ILO Convention On Freedom of Association and Protection of the Right to Organize, which states that the public authorities shall refrain from any interference which would restrict this right or impede the lawful exercise thereof (Article 2, Part 2).

464. The RF Law on Trade Unions (Article 8) stipulates that trade unions are recognized to be created from the moment a respective decision is taken. They are entitled to function without any registration as a legal entity. Such a registration itself must be carried out just by notification (in compliance with the legislation departments of justice must not be entitled to deny trade unions their registration on any grounds).

465. The reorganization or termination of activity of a trade union, as well as a primary (local) trade union organization shall be effected by the decision of its members, in the manner determined by the rules of the trade union and the statute of the primary trade union organization (Article 10 of the Law on Trade Unions).

The trade union may be prohibited only if its activity is contrary to the RF Constitution, the constitutions (charters) of RF subjects or federal laws. Such a trade union may be suspended for a period of up to six months or prohibited by decision of the RF Supreme Court, the court of an RF subject, or by the decision of Russian Procurator-General or the procurator of the respective RF subject.

466. Some indirect restrictions on the right to form and to join trade unions appeared after the LC was approved. In particular, the LC grants the rights to represent the interests of employees, including the right to collective bargaining and to participation in the settlement of collective labour disputes, mainly to local trade unions (primary trade union organizations). The local trade union means not just a trade union established at the level of an enterprise, but a trade union which is a part of a larger trade union guided by the charter of such larger trade union.

467. For the purposes of realizing their rights and freedoms, trade unions enjoy other legislative guarantees, including ones for the members of trade unions engaged in their management. These guarantees may cover all members of trade unions, as well as be granted for the members of elected trade union managing bodies. *See* paragraphs 404 and 405.

§3. Freedom Not to Join a Trade Union

468. Trade union membership is voluntary. The RF LC prohibits discrimination by reason of trade union affiliation or non-affiliation. The same proposal is included in the Law on Trade Unions.

In reality there are examples of interference in trade unions' right to make independent decisions related to their own activities. For instance, employers apply to courts with a claim to recognize trade unions' resolutions as unlawful and to argue against the establishment of trade unions and against provisions of their by-laws. Judicial proceedings in some of such cases last for three or four years, and judgments are revised many times. Quite often in new companies employers themselves initiate the establishment of a trade union under their control so as to prevent the creation of an independent trade union in future.

469. It is necessary to emphasize the fact that Russia lacks a mechanism for protecting employees from discrimination based on trade union membership and involvement in trade union activities. No remedies are available, while attempts to take discrimination complaints to court do not have any effect.

470. It should be also mentioned that the main function of trade unions is to represent and protect the rights and interests of trade union members in matters of individual labour relations and relations connected with labour. Therefore not to join a trade union may result in some limitations for an employee in the sphere of realization of his/her rights. At the same time in the field of collective rights and interests, trade unions represent the interests of employees, irrespective of trade union membership, in the event if they are vested with powers of representation in the established manner.

Chapter 2. The Trade Unions and Employers' Associations

§1. The Structure of Trade Unions

471. The Ministry of Justice of Russia has registered over 200 associations of trade unions in accordance with the notification registration procedure, which gives them the right to represent the interests of the trade union organizations they unite at federal level. There is a growing acceptance of the notion of three different groups of trade unions:

(1) Group one consists of the unions with large membership and well-developed structure that belong, for the most part, to the FNPR (*see* paragraphs 473 and 475).
(2) Group two includes so-called new unions, quite often based on the occupation principle and having weaker ties with the old structures (*Sotsprof*, the Independent Union of Miners, etc.).
(3) Group three covers trade unions that initially had representatives of the private sector cooperatives and small businesses as their members. Most important, they were represented by managers who had as their objectives not only to protect social interests of the unions' members, but to defend as well the very right to exist for certain forms of economic activities.

472. The RF Law on Trade Unions makes reference to the following types of trade unions:

(a) all-Russia trade union – a voluntary association of the trade union members of one or several spheres of activity, linked up by common social labour and occupational interests and operating across the entire territory of the RF or across the territory of over half of the subjects of the RF, or uniting not less than half of the total number of workers of one of several spheres of activity;
(b) all-Russia association of trade unions – a voluntary association of all-Russia trade unions, or of the territorial associations of the trade union organizations, operating across the entire territory of the RF or across the territory of over half of the subjects of the RF;
(c) interregional trade union – a voluntary association of the trade union members – the workers of one or of several spheres of activity, operating across the territory of not less than half of the subjects of the RF;
(d) interregional association of the trade union organizations – a voluntary association of the interregional trade unions and (or) of the territorial associations of the trade union organizations, operating across the territory of less than half of the subjects of the RF;
(e) territorial association of the trade union organizations – a voluntary association of trade union organizations, operating, as a rule, across the territory of one of the subjects of the RF or across the territory of a city or of a district; and
(f) territorial trade union association – a voluntary association of the members of local trade union organizations of one and the same trade union, operating

across the territory of one of the subjects of the RF, or across the territory of several subjects of the RF, or across the territory of a city or of a district.

473. The biggest trade union associations in Russia are the following:

- Russian Federation of Independent Trade Unions (*Federatsiya Nezavisimykh Profsouzov Rossii* – FNPR); and
- Confederation of Russian Labour (*Konfederatsiya Truda Rossii* – KTR);

All of them simultaneously became members of the International Confederation of Free Trade Unions in 1998.

474. During recent years the tendency of reducing of trade unions membership takes place. In 2016 their membership in the most important trade union organization–FNPR – was estimated as 20.7 million (in comparison to 2009, when there were 31.5 million members in FNPR). The KTR includes industry trade unions connected with sea transport (dockers, sailors, seaport workers), with other types of transport, for example railway (railway engine drivers), aviation, as well as several regional trade union associations. The All-Russian Confederation of Labour (VKT) comprised trade unions in coal and mining industries and regional trade union associations. There are many regional trade union associations which are not included in any of the above all-Russian organizations.

I. Russian Federation of Independent Trade Unions

475. The Federation of Independent Russian Trade Unions (FNPR) was founded in 1990. It is the largest from the point of view of number of members. It operates on the basis of its Charter independently from executive bodies of state power and public organizations. The FNPR enjoys an observer status at the UN Economic and Social Council. The FNPR budget is formed by membership dues paid by its member organizations, bank transfers, donations and profits of enterprises which belong to or have been instituted with the FNPR participation as well as other legal contributions. The Federation also gets its money from different actions which it organizes.

FNPR has a network for training trade union personnel. It actively cooperates with the ILO, as well as maintaining contacts with trade union centres in more than 100 foreign countries. Nineteen FNPR organizations are members of International Trade Union Secretariats.[196]

FNPR is very active in participating at legislative initiatives. During 2001–2003 trade unions, including FNPR, prepared and analysed legislative proposals concerning more than 400 draft laws.

196. <www.russiatoday.ru/en/politics/pol_sys/tr_un>.

II. The All-Russian Confederation of Labour

476. The VKT was founded in 1995 in Yekaterinburg to unite major trade unions that are not affiliated with the FNPR. The VKT was registered with the Russian Justice Ministry in the spring of 1996. In December 1999, the VKT became the member of the RTC. The VKT holds political and economic actions, some of which take radical forms. The Independent Miners' Union is one of its most active members.

III. The Confederation of Russian Labour

477. The KTR was founded in April 1995. It affiliated six national and four interregional trade unions and eight territorial trade union associations. It has regional branches. Though the KTR did not have representatives in the legislative bodies of state power, it was a member of the RTC. During the past decade the KTR has lost its practical importance, whereas some KTR members still play an active role in the activities of the International Transport Federation.

§2. The Role of Trade Unions

478. The two main functions of trade unions follow from Russian legislation:

(1) to protect the rights and interests of employees; and
(2) to represent employees.

I. To Protect Employees' Rights and Interests

479. Trade unions enjoy a wide range of rights in the sphere of the protection of employees' rights and representation of their interest in different spheres. First, trade unions participate in regulating of conditions of work at an enterprise level. Systems of labour remuneration, forms of material incentives, amounts of tariff rates (salaries) and also labour norms are established by employers and their amalgamations (unions, associations), by agreement with the respective trade union bodies.

480. Second, trade union representatives have the right to undertake some controlling functions. In particular they have unimpeded access to the organizations and workplaces where members of their trade unions work, for the purpose of implementing the statutory tasks and exercising the rights granted to trade unions. For the purpose of implementation of the supervision over the observance of the LC and other legal acts, containing labour regulations, the all-Russian trade unions and their associations can establish legal and technical trade union labour inspections. Interregional, as well as territorial alliance (association) of trade union organizations, acting on the territory of a subject of the RF, can establish legal and technical trade union labour inspections too.

Trade union labour inspectors, according to the procedures set, have the right to visit unhindered organizations, in which members of a given trade union or trade unions, forming part of an association, are employed, with the purpose of inspecting the observance of the labour legislation, as well as compliance with the provisions of the collective agreement.

481. Liquidation of an organization and its divisions, change in the form of property or the legal organization form of an organization, full or partial suspension of production (work) entailing a reduction in the quantity of workplaces or a worsening of working conditions may be effected only after preliminary notification (at least three months in advance) of the respective trade unions and the holding with them of negotiations on observance of the rights and interests of trade union members.[197]

482. In some cases the RF LC requires that an employer should make decisions with due consideration of the opinion of respective trade union body. This procedure is stipulated by the LC (Article 372). *See also* paragraph 329.

Regarding definite situations, the consideration of motivated opinion of an elective trade union body is demanded. In particular it concerns some cases of termination of contracts of employment with members of a trade union, initiated by the employer (Article 373 of the RF LC).

II. To Represent Employees

483. Today in the overwhelming majority of cases, trade unions and their associations perform the function of employees' authorized representatives in the process of collective bargaining and working out collective agreements.

484. In the sphere of representing employees, the trade unions may take part in the consideration of their proposals by the organs of state power, organs of local self-government, and also by employers, their unions and associations and other public entities.

In accordance with the law 'On the RTC',[198] each of the all-Russia associations of trade unions can delegate a representative to the Commission. They also have the right to increase, within the limits prescribed by the law (thirty seats for each social partner in the Commission), the number of their representatives in proportion to the number of the trade unions they unite.

197. *See* para. 398.
198. The RF Law No. 92 'On Russian Tripartite Commission for Regulation of Social and Labour Relations' of 1 May 1999.

§3. The Employers' Organizations

485. At present it is possible to identify several groups of associations of subjects of economic activity, which have defined as their charter objective representation of the interests of their members in the labour relations regulatory processes and in dealing with trade unions and the state. They are the following:

(1) non-commercial unions and associations of industrialists and businessmen established on the basis of former public associations and operating at federal, regional and territorial levels;
(2) Russian joint-stock companies within certain industries, entrusted by the enterprises and subsidiaries they unite to represent, through their administrative bodies, their interests as employers;
(3) the Chamber of Commerce and Industry of the RF and its regional offices; and
(4) executive authority bodies acting as employers' representatives.

More than twenty associations represent today employers on the RTC. The Chamber of Commerce and Industry of the RF is also represented on the Commission.

I. The Chamber of Commerce and Industry (CCI)

486. The All-Union Chamber of Commerce and Industry was established on 28 May 1932. Its articles of association stipulated assistance to companies in the development of domestic trade. The All-Union CCI establishes business ties with foreign commercial and business organizations, received foreign business delegations and sent Soviet trade and industrial delegations abroad.

In March 1972, the All-Union Chamber of Commerce and Industry was transformed into the USSR Chamber of Commerce and Industry. The Chamber's functions included assistance in exports development, consulting services, establishment and development of contacts with foreign business communities and general public, the study, summarizing and distribution of reference and information literature on economics and expert examination.

In October 1991, the Chamber of Commerce and Industry of the Russian Federation (RF CCI) was established. The Chamber's goals and objectives included protection of interests in the area of business activities.

II. The Russian Union of Industrialists and Entrepreneurs

487. In the early 1990th twenty-four people's deputies appealed to the public to form a union that would protect the common interests of the industries and science. The purpose of such a new non-political organization was to create parity between the Government, trade unions and industries proper in a time of rapid and sweeping changes in Government, politics and the economy. The appeal was enthusiastically supported. In June 1990 the Science and Industrial Union was founded.

In December 1991, the Russian Union of Industrialists and Entrepreneurs (RSPP) was founded. During 1992–2000, the efforts of this organization were concentrated, *inter alia*, at developing proposals in the economic and social areas.

In 2000–2001, changes within the country and ensuing economic changes made for a new status of the RSPP. It began consolidating forces for supporters of structural reforms in economic and social policies.

488. Currently the RSPP unites prominent managers, researches and public figures. To date, more than 328,000 representatives of industrial, financial, research and consultative organizations from all parts of the country that in total count for more than 80% of national GDP have been granted RSPP membership. Collaboration with governmental bodies and trade unions, and development of the system of social partnership, is named as one of the main goals of its activity.[199]

III. The Coordinating Council of Employers' Unions of Russia

489. The main role in the sphere of labour relationships belongs to the Coordinating Council of Employers' Unions of Russia (CCEUR). It is a non-profit organization that consolidates employers and their unions (associations) in their efforts to influence the formation of social and economic policies.

The predecessor of the CCEUR – the Coordinating Council of Employers' Unions – was founded in November 1994. In March 2000, the Coordinating Council was transformed into a non-profit organization with the name of the 'Coordinating Council of Employers' Unions of Russia' (CCEUR).

490. At present the CCEUR comprises twenty-nine member organizations that represent Russian employers and their unions, in particular the following:

- Russian Union of Industrialists and Entrepreneurs (RSPP);
- Union of Public Associations of Entrepreneurs and Renters of Russia;
- Employers' Union of Russian Engineering;
- Union of Russian Ship-Owners;
- Union of Industrialists and Entrepreneurs of Coal-Mining Industry;
- Moscow Chamber of Commerce and Industry;
- Congress of Russian Business Circles;
- Association of Industrialists of the Mining and Steel-Making Industry of Russia;
- Russian Union of Constructors;
- All-Russia Association of Privatized and Private Enterprises;
- Association of Joint Ventures, International Unions and Organizations;
- All-Russia Union of Entrepreneurs of Small and Medium Business; and
- Non-profit Organization 'Association of Air Navigation Service'.

199. <www.rspp.biz/eng>.

491. In the sphere of social partnership, the role of employers' associations is defined by RF Law No. 156-FZ of 27 November 2002 'On Employers' Associations', applied with subsequent amendments, and the most recent of them were of 28 November 2015. Among the functions of these associations are the following:

(1) consolidation of employers and their associations for the purposes of influencing the process of formation of social and economic policies;
(2) coordination of actions by employers and their associations in the areas of employment policy, wages, occupational safety and social insurance of employees;
(3) contribution to developing and strengthening a socially oriented market economy system and a system of social partnership;
(4) improvement and development of the legal basis of socio-labour and economic relations;
(5) ensuring the participation of Russian employers in the activities of international organizations;
(6) coordination and representation of interests of employers and their associations in the process of concluding General Agreements;[200]
(7) providing expert assessment of draft legislation dealing with issues of social, labour and economic relations, state employment programmes and occupational safety;
(8) participation of CCEUR experts in the implementation of various federal programmes, including tax and pension reforms;
(9) organizing and conducting seminars, conferences and internships on the issues of social and labour relations;
(10) establishing and maintaining bilateral contacts with employers' associations of foreign countries; and
(11) participation on behalf of Russian employers in the activities of the International Organization of Employers, ILO and other international organizations.

200. *See* para. 533.

Chapter 3. Institutionalized Relations Between Employers and Employees

492. The relations among employees (representatives of employees) and employers (representatives of employers) constitute the system of social partnership in Russia.[201]

493. The RF LC establishes the following forms of social partnership:[202]

- collective bargaining for the preparation of draft collective contracts, agreements and their conclusion;
- mutual consultations (negotiations) on issues of labour relations and other relations directly linked to them, on safeguarding guarantees of employees' labour rights and on improving the LLs;
- participation of employees and their representatives in managing an organization (the enterprise); and
- participation of employees' and employers' representatives in settlement of labour disputes.

§1. Workers' Participation at the Enterprise Level

I. Local Trade Union Organizations and Other Workers' Representative Bodies

494. The workers' right to participate in the management of the enterprise (plant, establishment) directly or through their representative bodies is ensured in the LC (Article 52), other federal laws, collective agreements and enterprise level regulations. Main forms of workers' participation are the following:

(a) taking account by the employer of the opinion of the workers' representative body in cases specifically envisaged in the LC or collective agreements;[203]
(b) employer's consultations with the workers' representatives on the matters concerning the adoption of the local normative legal acts;
(c) participation of the workers' representatives in collective bargaining; and
(d) other forms provided for by the LC, collective agreements or enterprise level regulations (Article 53 of the LC).

495. Under Russian LL, the interests of employees may be represented by trade unions, as well as by other representative bodies.

The legal status of trade unions (including the establishment, the role and structure) is quite clearly defined by legislation. *See* paragraphs 478–482.

---

201. *See also* paras 74–76 and 129.
202. Article 27 of the RF LC.
203. *For instance, see* para. 347.

The status, as well as the structure of other representative bodies, does not directly stem from the legislation. They may be called differently (e.g., workers' counsels). The establishment and the structure thereof is mostly defined by their participants. The competence is followed from the legislation. In particular the RF LC quite often makes reference to workers' representative bodies alongside trade unions. *See also* paragraph 521.

496. It should be noted that some spheres of regulation may be realized only with participation of trade unions, whereas regarding other spheres legislation does not have special requirement of the type of the representative which may participate. For instance, an employer issues local normative acts containing the LL norms within the limits of its competence. In cases stipulated by the legislation, as well as by collective agreements, an employer shall take into account the opinion of the workers' representing body (Article 8 of the RF LC).

II. Labour Protection Services and Commissions

497. The RF LC (the version of 2006) requires that a labour protection service shall be set up in every organization performing production activities with over fifty employees. Otherwise the position of a labour protection expert with appropriate training or work experience in this field shall be established.

In the enterprises with the number of employees of fifty or fewer, the decision about the formation of the labour protection service shall be taken by the employer with regard for the features peculiar to this organization's activities.

The structure of the labour protection service in the organization, as well as the number of specialists involved, shall be determined by the employer with regard for the recommendations of the federal state authority (the MLSP).[204]

498. For the purposes of observing of labour protection requirements and prevention of industrial accidents and occupational diseases, labour protection committees/commissions shall be set up in organizations (enterprises). It is important to stress that current legislation provides the establishment of such committees not only by the employers' initiative, but also by the initiative of employees or their representative body.

Labour protection committees/commissions also organize and conduct inspections of the working conditions and health protection, inform employees on the results of these inspections, etc.[205]

III. Commissions on Collective Bargaining

499. Commissions which are formed for the purpose of collective bargaining and conclusion of collective agreements are based on the equality principle.

---

204. Article 217 of the RF LC.
205. Article 218 of the RF LC.

Persons participating in bargaining, including specially invited experts, receive certain guarantees and compensations. They retain their regular jobs and wages for a period of up to three months annually. All the expenditures incurred due to their participation in bargaining shall be compensated according to the order fixed by labour legislation. The exact procedure of compensation can be described in the relative collective agreement. Members of such commissions enjoy additional guarantees in the sphere of labour legislation.[206]

500. The establishment of collective bargaining commissions is regulated by labour legislation, as well as by the participants of the bargaining. For instance, commissions' membership, place of negotiations and agenda are agreed upon by the negotiating parties (the appropriate written decision is required). If there are several representatives of employees, they shall within five calendar days form a single representative body for carrying out negotiations, developing a single draft collective agreement and signing it. In absence of such a single body representing workers, general meeting (conference) of workers has the right to approve the draft collective agreement worked out by the workers' representative they find most acceptable and empower that representative with the right to negotiate on their behalf with employer's representative. In case of failure to reach an agreement between workers' representatives on setting up a single body, they have the right to bargain and conclude a collective agreement on behalf of employees they represent or to propose a supplement to the single collective agreement.

IV. Labour Dispute Commissions

501. For the purposes of individual labour disputes resolving, Labour Dispute Commissions are established. They may be formed at the initiative of employees and (or) employer. The LDC consists of representatives of employees and employer in equal numbers. Representatives of employees are elected to the labour dispute commission by the general meeting (conference) of employees of an organization or are delegated by the representative body of employees with subsequent approval by the general meeting (conference) of employees of an organization.

By the resolution of the general meeting of employees, labour dispute commissions can be formed in structural departments of an organization.

502. The LDC processes individual labour disputes arising in organizations, with the exception of disputes, for which another processing procedure is set by the LC and other federal laws (for instance, disputes on termination of employment, which are directly resolved in court, without preliminary procedure).

An individual labour dispute is processed by the labour dispute commission if an employee in the course of direct discussion with an employer does not solve the differences himself/herself or with the participation of his/her representative.

206. *See* para. 413.

503. Labour legislation provides the principles of social partnership in the sphere of establishing of the bodies aimed at collective labour dispute settlement.[207]

§2. Social Partnership at Other Levels

I. Russian Tripartite Commission

504. In respect of collective bargaining at the level of the Federation, the most important role is vested to the RTC of the RF.[208]

Apart from conducting negotiations and ensuring control over the agreement fulfilment, the commission has a range of other functions within its competence:

(a) to promote bargaining at federal level;
(b) to carry out consultations on developing draft federal laws and other legal instruments of the RF in the sphere of labour relations, federal programmes in employment, workforce migration and social support; and
(c) to inform other commissions (e.g., branch/inter-branch and regional commissions on regulation of social and labour relations) about its activities and some others.

II. Tripartite Commissions in Subjects of the RF

505. In the majority of the subjects of the RF, tripartite commissions are established on a permanent basis. They represent the main tool promoting social dialogue. Their activities are regulated by the legislation of the subjects of the RF, including laws on social partnership. For example, the Law of Sverdlovsk Region 'On Social Partnership' defines that territorial commissions might be established to cooperate with the Regional Tripartite Commission following a relevant agreement. Thus the main aim of establishment of such commissions is defined as cooperation with the regional commission for regulating social and labour relations, but not the settlement of labour and social issues on the spot. The right of the subjects of economic activities for free and absolutely independent bargaining position and for establishing commissions for this purpose is violated.[209]

III. Institutions Established for Collective Dispute Settlement

506. Some institutions based on social partnership principles are established to the settlement of collective labour disputes at the above analysed level.[210]

207. *See* paras 590 and 606.
208. *See* paras 129 and 160.
209. *See also* para. 518.
210. *See also* paras 606–607.

Chapter 4. Collective Bargaining

§1. Interpretation and Historical Development

507. In accordance with the LC, Russian LL regulations aim to guarantee a balance of interests between employees and employers. Collective bargaining plays an important role in the achieving of this aim.

The notion of collective bargaining in Russian LL is connected to the widely used term 'social partnership'. As a rule, the term 'social partnership' implies presenting the results of negotiations in the form of documents that fix the agreed balance of interests. Russian labour legislation recognizes social partnership as one of its fundamental principles (Article 2 of the RF LC).[211]

508. The collective bargaining process in Russia began to be regulated by law after the revolution of 1917. The first Russian (Soviet) LC (1918) envisaged regulation through collective agreements to be developed at enterprise level by the trade unions, in cooperation with enterprise managements.

The LC of 1922 and its later versions defined a collective agreement as the agreement concluded between a trade union (as workers' representatives), on the one hand, and the employer, on the other hand. The agreement was aimed to determine conditions of hire and work for specific enterprises and institutions or groups of such and the content of individual contracts of employment. Mostly collective agreements contained obligations of employers in respect to employees. Throughout the 1920s, they were full-fledged documents defining interactions of the parties to labour relations.

From 1934 to 1947 collective bargaining practice did not exist. Later on, until the end of 1980s, the content and principles of concluding of collective agreements had fundamental differences from real agreements. To a large extent, collective agreements were a specific tool of social regulation under the planned economy conditions.

509. Radical changes in ownership relations, and the increased independence of employees' organizations from the state and from employers, were some of the objective preconditions to the development of a system of social partnership in 1990th. As a consequence, a new legal framework for the regulation of social and labour relations, through the bargaining process, has emerged.

The term 'social partnership' appeared in the Presidential Decree of 15 November 1991 'On Social Partnership and Settlement of Labour Disputes'. The Decree has become one of the first legal acts in modern history aimed at developing agreement-based regulation of social and labour relations. In 1992 the RF Law 'On Collective Agreements' was adopted.[212]

211. *See also* paras 74–76.
212. The RF Law No. 2490-1 of 11 Mar. 1992 'On Collective Agreements', with subsequent additions and amendments.

510. The process of arranging the system of collective bargaining of the RF was connected to establishing the RTC, in accordance with the Presidential Decree of 25 January 1992. The status of the Commission as a permanent body is currently defined by the RF LC (Article 35) and the RF Law 'On Russian Tripartite Commission for Regulation of Social and Labour Relations' of 1 May 1999 No. 92. Among its other functions arepromotion of the regulation of social and labour relations at federal level; carrying out consultations on issues related to the elaboration of draft federal laws and other normative acts of the RF on social and labour relations, etc.[213]

511. The activities of tripartite commissions of the RF subjects are regulated by regional legislation, including laws on social partnership. Around thirty subjects of the RF adopted their laws on tripartite commissions.

512. The current LC is seen as a compromise between social partners – employers, employees and state authorities.

The RF LC stipulates the right of an employee to take part in the managing and organizing of the labour process. To initiate the bargaining, as well as to participate in it, is of the sides of this right (Article 21 of LC).[214]

513. Social partnership is regulated at the level of subjects of the RF too. Laws on social partnership are issued in more than sixty subjects of the RF.

514. In many respects the legal basis for social partnership in Russia has been formed under the influence of rules developed by the international community, first of all by ILO Conventions and Recommendations on the promotion of collective bargaining and freedom of association. In particular, the ILO Convention 98 'On the Right to Organize and Conduct Collective Bargaining' was ratified by the RF.

515. Collective bargaining is based on the fundamental right of freedom of association, which primarily flows from the RF Constitution. Basic principles of governing the conclusion of collective agreements also include equality between the representatives of the parties, freedom of choice and discussion of matters likely to be covered by collective agreements, financial guarantees of the obligations adopted, control and supervision and assumption of responsibility.[215]

§2. Levels of Collective Bargaining

516. In accordance with the RF LC, the system of the social partnership must include the following levels:[216]

---

213. *See also* paras 129 and 160.
214. *See also* paras 500 and 501.
215. *See also* paras 158–160.
216. Article 26 of the RF LC.

(a) the federal level setting the grounds for regulating relations in the sphere of labour in the RF;
(b) the interregional level where the grounds for regulating relations in the sphere of labour in two and more subjects of the RF are established;
(c) the regional level setting the grounds for regulating relations in the sphere of labour in a subject of the RF;
(d) the industry (branch) level in the sphere of labour in a particular industry (or several industries);
(e) the territorial level establishing the principles of regulating relations in the sphere of labour in a municipal division; and
(f) the local level (an enterprise, plant, organization) where specific mutual obligations in the sphere of labour between the employees and the employer are established.

517. All of these levels may be represented by collective agreements.

The LC defines 'collective agreement' in its narrow sense as a legal act to regulate the social-labour relations between the employer and the employees of an enterprise and its representation by an independent body (Article 40). Collective agreements are recognized as sources of LL. They may be a range of levels and, by decision of the parties to the negotiations, such agreements may be tripartite or bilateral.

518. In 2000 together with one General Agreement, 61 federal industry level agreements, 77 regional level agreements, 2,293 regional industry level agreements and 161,700 collective agreements at an enterprise level were concluded in the RF.[217]

By 2018 80 regional level agreements, 60 branch and more than 4,000 regional and other territorial branch agreements were concluded in the RF.[218]

See also paragraph 519.

I. Local (Enterprise, Plant, Company, etc.) Level

519. Being concluded at an enterprise level, collective agreements may play the role of so-called constitutions within an enterprise. They may establish rules for remuneration and other terms of work, social guarantees (included ones which deal with social security) and privileges for employees.

Collective agreements resolved at company level are viewed as quite widespread in the RF. For instance according to data provided by the RF MLSD (currently – the MLSP), the total number of collective agreements concluded in 2001 increased by 10% as compared to 2000; in 2002 the number of collective agreements increased by 3.57% as compared to 2001. By the end of 2003, the total number of collectiveagreements concluded at the enterprise level was estimated as 182,000.

217. National weekly newspaper *Economika i Jizn*, March 2001, No. 9.
218. Data provided by FNPR, *see*//www.fnpr..ru.

The data provided by FNPR show that in 2006, the total number of collective agreements was accounted as 184,265 which include 84.76% of all members of trade union organizations at enterprises. Consequently around 24,295,000 employees were covered by collective agreements.[219]

520. It should be noted that there is no obligation of an employer to regulate internal labour relationships within the company by collective agreements. A relevant obligationarises in the case if the initiative of employees (or their representative) appeared.

Each of the parties to a collective agreement is entitled to take the initiative for collective bargaining in order to prepare, conclude or revise this legal act. Any party that has been notified in writing by the other party of the initiative of the latter one shall begin such negotiations within a definite period of time (seven days).

521. The concept of employees' representatives has to be seen in the light of the LC. In accordance with the LC, the right to conduct collective bargaining on behalf of employees is delegated to trade unions represented by their competent bodies. Employees may be also represented by other bodies (e.g., workers' councils elected at the general meeting of employees, if a trade union organization does not exist, or if a trade union covers less than half of the employees). In practice employees are usually represented by trade unions.

522. In accordance with Russian legislation, collective bargaining on behalf of employers can be carried out by leaders of enterprises (organizations) and other persons duly authorized under the organization's charter and other legal acts, as well as by the authorized bodies of employers' associations (Article 33 of LC). The legal status of the representatives is defined in more detail by special legislation (e.g., legislation on joint-stock companies).

II. Industry (Inter-industry) Level

523. At the level of industry (of several industries), branch (inter-branch) collective agreements may be concluded; sixty branch collective agreements have been concluded with participation of state bodies by the beginning of 2018.[220]

The parties to such agreements are the relevant all-Russia trade unions and their associations, all-Russia employers' associations (other duly authorized employers' representative bodies) and the MLSP of the RF or an appropriate state body (e.g., a branch collective agreement to regulate relevant relations within federal railway transport was concluded for the period 2001–2003 with the participation of the Ministry of Transport of the RF). Tripartite collective agreements were also signed in the mining industry (with participation of the Russian Independent Trade Union of

219. *Ibid.*
220. *Ibid.*

Miners); in the car industry (with participation of the RF Association of Car Industry Trade Unions); and in textiles and light industry (with participation of the Russian Trade Union of Workers of Textile and Light Industry).

III. Regional, Interregional and Territorial Collective Agreements

524. Regional collective agreements establish the general principles of regulation of social-labour relations in the RF at the level of subjects of the RF. One of the parties to the agreements is the executive authority body of the subjects of the Federation.

525. Currently regional agreements are mostly concluded on a tripartite basis. By the beginning of 2018 around 80 tripartite regional agreements were signed.[221] Within the regions of the RF, territorial agreements may be concluded. Usually they include working standards and social guarantees depending on the special characteristics of particular cities, districts and other administrative-territorial units. One of the parties to such agreements is the appropriate body of local self-government.

By the end of 2017, more than 4,000 branch and territorial agreements in the subjects of the RF were concluded. But somewhere territorial agreements are not signed on grounds of the absence of employers' associations (e.g., Magadan).

IV. General Agreements

526. The highest level of collective agreements is represented by the General Agreement, which is concluded between the state (the Government of the RF), all-Russian associations of employers and Russian association of trade unions. A General Agreement establishes basic principles to regulate social relations at federal level. Current General Agreement was concluded for the period of 2018–2020.

§3. Content of Bargaining

527. The content and structure of a collective agreement is to be determined by the parties which have a certain degree of freedom in this respect. In particular, they may choose to include mutual obligations in collective agreements.

The RF LC suggests that the following mutual obligations of an employer and employees may be fixed in a collective agreement:

- forms, schedules and amounts of remuneration;
- payment of bonuses, premiums, compensations;
- mechanism of regulating wages with account for rising prices, inflation level;
- employment, retraining, conditions of employees' dismissal;

221. *Ibid.*

- working and rest time including the granting of leave and its duration;
- improvement of working conditions and occupational safety, including those for women and young people;
- environmental safety and occupational health of production employees;
- guarantees and benefits to employees combining work with study;
- control of the realization of collective agreement, procedures of amending and appending it, liability of the parties, ensuring normal conditions for functioning of employees' representatives;
- renunciation of strikes in case of realizing of the appropriate terms of the collective agreement; and
- other matters as determined by the parties.[222]

528. In respect of the content of a collective agreement, it is necessary to mention that Russian labour legislation stipulates some limitations to the principle of freedom of contracts. No collective agreement may reduce the level of guarantees stated by legislations. Clauses of collective agreements which are less favourable than legislative provisions in respect of the situation of employees are null and void.

The RF LC also makes reference to basic principles of social partnership (e.g., equality between the representatives of the parties; freedom of choice and discussion of matters likely to be covered by collective agreements; etc.). One of the principles stated is providing of financial guarantees of the obligations adopted. With taking into account this requirement an employer only has the right to establish at its own expense, additional social privileges for all employees or some categories of employees.

529. Representatives of employees and employers are entitled to take initiatives on engaging in collective bargaining. Representatives of the party receiving a written notification proposing to commence collective bargaining shall enter into the bargaining within seven calendar days after the reception date for the notification.[223]

530. The procedures of preparing the draft collective contract and concluding it shall be determined by the parties in accordance with legislation (mainly the RF LC). In this respect the most important is to solve the situation in case of the existence of several trade unions at the enterprise (local trade unions). The current LC introduced the new provision which is applied in such situations. In particular, in case if there are two or more trade union local organizations operate within an enterprise, they may form a unified representative body for engaging in collective bargaining, preparing a single draft collective contract and concluding it. Formation of a unified representative body shall be done on the basis of the proportional representation principle depending on the number of the trade union members. A representative shall be delegated from each local trade union organization. The local

222. *See also* paras 33, 287, 406, 421 and 456.
223. Article 36 of the RF LC.

trade union amalgamating over half of the employees may begin the collective bargaining procedure on behalf of all employees without formation of a unified representative body.

If no local trade union amalgamates over half of the employees, the employees' general meeting (conference) shall determine by a secret vote the local trade union entrusted with forming the representative body or starting of collective negotiations. In both of these cases, other local trade unions have the right to delegate their representatives to the representative body prior to the moment of signing the collective agreement.[224]

The right to be engaged in collective bargaining and sign agreements on behalf of the employees at other levels (e.g., the RF level; at the level of a subject of the RF; as well as within an industry or a territory) shall be granted to relevant trade union (or trade union association). If several trade unions exist at the relevant level, each of them shall be entitled to representation within a unified representative body for collective bargaining formed with account for the number of trade union members they represent. In the absence of an agreement on establishing a unified representative body for collective bargaining, the right to engage in it shall be granted to the trade union (association) amalgamating the largest number of the trade union members.

531. Persons participating in collective bargaining, including specially invited experts, receive certain guarantees and compensation. They retain their regular jobs and wages for a period of up to three months annually. All the expenditures incurred due to their participation in bargaining are compensated according to the order fixed by labour legislation. Exact procedure of compensation can be described in the relative collective agreement.

Representatives of trade unions and their associations shall not be subject to any disciplinary measure, transfer to another job or dismissal on the management initiative while they are engaged in the negotiation process. *See also* paragraph 406.

§4. Binding Effect

I. General Validation

532. Russian legislation stipulates that the terms of collective agreements concluded in accordance with legislation apply to all the employees they cover. It is also presumed that collective agreements cover employees within a traditional employment relationship.[225]

The legislation makes no reference to other workers (self-employed, temporary workers, etc.) with respect to their rights in collective bargaining. Therefore the

224. Article 37 of the RF LC.
225. *See also* paras 69 and 70.

problem of social protection of so-called atypical employment (including temporary workers involved in relationships with private employment agencies) has not been given the attention it needs. In general such workers are not covered by collective agreements.

II. The Relations Between Individual Employment Contracts and Collective Agreements

533. The role of collective agreements is clearly defined in compliance with the principle of conformity of the collective agreement and contract of employment, with legislation.[226]

534. It is also inadmissible to include into individual contracts of employment less favourable terms than provided for by the corresponding terms of collective agreements and legislation. Such clauses of contracts of employment shall be null and void.

III. The Duration of Collective Agreements

535. Russian legislation limits the maximum duration of collective agreements to three years (Article 43 of LC). Collective agreements come into force at the time of signature by the parties, or from the date fixed by the agreement. On the expiry of the fixed time limit, the collective agreement shall remain in force until the parties conclude a new collective agreement, or amend or supplement the agreement in force.

IV. Registration

536. Collective agreements have to be registered in the MLSP. It should be noted that the fact of such registration does not influence the binding force of an agreement. The purpose of the registration is supervision of the application of a collective agreement.

§5. Extension

537. The collective agreement concluded within an enterprise (its division, etc.) cover all the employees of the organization, its subsidiary, representative office and other separate structural division.

---

226. *See also* para. 535.

538. A collective agreement retains its validity in case of change in composition, structure or name of the managing body of the organization. A collective agreement remains in force during any period of restructuring of an enterprise, institution or organization and can be revised afterwards on the initiative of any of the parties. In case of liquidation procedures opened against an enterprise, the collective agreement remains in force for the whole period of liquidation procedures. In case of the transfer of a business, the collective agreement retains its validity for a period of three months, following which the workers and the employer must make a decision on extending its validity or beginning collective bargaining over a new one.

539. Collective agreements concluded at upper levels (e.g., branch, interbranch, regional, interregional and territorial) cover the employees and employers who have authorized representatives of the parties at the collective bargaining to prepare and conclude it on their behalf, the state authority bodies and the self-government bodies within the limits of the obligations assumed by them as well as the employees and employers joining it after its conclusion.

540. If the employees are covered in the proper manner by several agreements, the terms of the agreement most favourable to them shall be effective.

541. As regards employers, such agreements cover all of them belonging to the association of employers concluding the agreement. Cancellation of its membership in the association of employers shall not relieve the employer from obligation to follow the agreement concluded during its membership period. The employer joining the association of employers within the period of the agreement validity shall realize the obligations stipulated by such agreement.

542. Article 48 of the RF LC provides that in cases where the branch (industry) collective agreement was concluded at the Federal level, the Federal Executive State Body, which has the function of legal regulation in the field of labour (the MLSP) has a right to offer the employers who have not participated in concluding this agreement to join it. If the employers, within thirty calendar days after official publication of the proposal to join the agreement, fail to submit to the federal executive authority body in the sphere of labour their written reasonable refusal to join it, the agreement shall be deemed to cover such employers as of the day of the proposal official publication.

Chapter 5. Strikes, Lockouts and Other Legal Forms of Industrial Action

§1. General Remarks

543. Strikes during Soviet time were not supported either by the policy of the state, or by legislation. In spite of that they sometimes happen.

544. At the end of 1980s, many strikes and other industrial actions occurred. As a consequence the relevant legislation was adopted. The first law regulating industrial actions in the USSR was issued in October 1989. It was the law 'On Regulation of Settlement of Collective Labour Disputes (Conflicts)'. Until the time when Russia passed its own legislation regarding collective dispute settlement, the above lawwas applied, as well as some other normative acts (such as the Decree of the President of the RF of 15 November 1991 'On Social Partnership and Settlement of Labour Disputes').

545. In 1995 the RF Law 'On Procedure of Settlement of Collective Labour Disputes'[227] (hereinafter – the Law on Settlement of Collective Disputes) was adopted. This law regulated the possible means applied for settlement of collective labour disputes, as well as the procedures of realization of the right to strike in the RF. At the same time, other industrial actions (such as collective protection of individual labour rights) were not covered by this law. The Supreme Court of the RF recognized such collective actions (e.g., mass terminating of work caused by non-paying of salaries to the employees engaged) as not being regulated by the law on collective disputes.[228] In this respect it has to be mentioned that the RF LC provides employees with the possibility to protect their rights in such situations by other means. In particular in case of delay in payment of a salary for the period exceeding fifteen days, having submitted a written notification to the employer, the employee has the right to suspend work for the whole period until the payment of the delayed sum. Suspension of work is not allowed in some cases (such as in periods of introducing the state of emergency, martial law or special measures in accordance with the laws on the state of emergency; etc.).[229]

546. The Law on Settlement of Collective Disputes was mostly incorporated by the current LC which contains a separate chapter (61) regulating consideration of collective industrial disputes. But the above law was still applicable in accordance with the Article 423 of the LC which reads that until harmonization of laws and other normative legal acts existing in the territory of the RF with the LC, the laws and mentioned acts are applicable insofar as they do not contravene to the LC. In force until October 2006, it is no longer applied.

227. The RF Law No. 175-FZ of 23 Nov. 1995 'On Procedure of Settlement of Collective Labour Disputes' (with subsequent alterations and additions, mainly in 2001).
228. Bulletin of the Supreme Court of the RF, 1998, No. 10.
229. Article 142 of the RF LC.

547. The right to strike is guaranteed by the RF Constitution (Article 37) which recognizes the right to individual and collective labour disputes and allows resolving them in ways by federal law, including the right to strike.

548. Under Russian LL the strike is defined as a temporary voluntary refusal of employees to perform their labour duties (wholly or in part) for the purpose of settlement of a collective industrial dispute (Article 398 of the LC).

549. The term 'lockout' is also used by Russian labour law. The RF LC provides the definition of this term as 'a dismissal of employees at the initiative of an employer in connection with their participation in the collective industrial dispute or strike'. Russian law prohibits lockouts throughout all the period of settlement of a collective industrial dispute, including the conduct of a strike (Article 415 of the LC).

550. It should be noted that in 2006 the RF LC added a reference to such forms of industrial actions as meetings and demonstrations. They may be used by employees (their representatives) as additional means to support their requirements during a particular collective dispute, including strikes (Article 401 of the RF LC).

§2. The Procedure for and the Consequences of Strikes

551. The RF LC requires that participation in a strike is voluntary. The voluntary character of strikes is guaranteed by responsibility in case of forcing of employees to participate at a strike, as well as compensations for employees, unable to do their work because of the strike and having stated in writing the beginning of a work stoppage, which shall be paid on the basis of no fault of employee, in the amount stipulated herein (of at least three-thirds of the tariff rates they are entitled to).[230]

552. Employees or their representatives are entitled to start a strike, if conciliatory procedures fail to settle a collective industrial dispute, or the employer evades conciliatory procedures or to perform the agreement reached in the course of the settlement of a collective industrial dispute.

553. A strike is called on the basis of the decision of a general meeting of the employees of an enterprise (organization, subsidiary, representative office, other separate structural subdivision) upon proposal submitted by duly authorized unit of employees. It is necessary to stress that the right to initiate the strike belongs only to the representative body of employees which was authorized previously to participate at settlement of the collective dispute. In this respect the adoption of the new RF LC made the legislative situation more problematic, since the provisions regulating the procedures of initiating a collective labour dispute and going on strike became more complicated. While previously this right was conferred both on employees of an organization as a whole and on trade unions, currently the LC

230. Article 409 of the RF LC.

stipulates that the trade union must obtain an approval of its decision by a majority vote of all employees of this organization at a meeting or conference. To take into account that many enterprises have thousands of employees, this provision is often impossible to comply with, for example, in case of protecting the interests of employees of a certain occupation in a single trade union (e.g., air traffic controllers and pilots).

The LC refers to the content of the decision of calling a strike, which, in particular, must incorporate proposals on the minimum of required accomplishments (services) to be carried out within an organization, subsidiary and other separate structural subdivision during the strike period.

554. The employer shall be given a written notice of a future strike not later than ten calendar days in advance. At the same time, the employer engaged shall notify the Service for Settlement of Collective Industrial Disputes about the forthcoming strike.

555. During the strike period, the parties to a collective industrial dispute shall be liable to continue the settlement of such dispute through the conduct of conciliatory procedures.

556. Among the duties of the parties to a collective dispute is also an obligation to provide the list of the minimum of required accomplishments (services) during the strike.

The LC states that the list of the minimum of required accomplishments (services) in organizations, subsidiaries, representative offices, whose activities are connected with safety of population, health support and essential public interests (so-called essential services) shall be produced and approved in each branch (sub-branch) of economy by federal executive body authorized for coordination and governing of activities in the respective branch (sub-branch) of economy. 'Rules on Establishing and Approving of Lists of the Minimum Required Accomplishments (Services)' were issued by the RF Government on 17 December 2002. The appropriate list also exists in the sphere of education.

The executive state bodies of subjects of the RF approve, on the basis of the above list, and upon the agreement with the respective territorial associations of trade unions, territorial lists of the minimum of required accomplishments in case of strikes.

The minimum of required accomplishments (services) in organization (subsidiary, other division) shall be determined upon the agreement of the parties to collective dispute, with participation of the appropriate local government.

557. The law characterizes a strike as illegal on rather a wide range of grounds. In particular the following strikes may be recognized as unlawful:

(1) strikes that began during the period of military or emergency situations or special procedures in accordance with the legislation on emergency situation;

(2) strikes in spheres where they are prohibited by law (such as at the bodies and organizations of the armed forces of the RF, military, militarized or other formations and organizations providing for the country defence, state safety, repair-rescuing, search-rescuing, and anti-fire operations, prevention or elimination of the Acts of God and emergency situations; in law enforcement bodies; and in organizations dealing with highly hazardous facilities or machinery, at ambulance stations of first medical aid);
(3) strikes in essential public services (energy, heating, water, gas supply, air, railway and water transport) in case the conduct of such strikes threaten the defence of the country and the life and health of its people;
(4) strikes announced without considering the terms, procedures and requirements of collective industrial dispute, stipulated herein.

558. The strike right may be also limited by federal laws. For instance strikes are prohibited for some employees of the railway transport.[231]

559. Courts are entitled, on the basis of the employer's or public prosecutor's claim, to find a strike illegal or to pass a judgment on postponing (or suspending) the strike. In particular, such cases may be resolved by Supreme Courts of republics, regional courts, municipal federal courts and courts of autonomous regions. Therefore the courts of general jurisdiction of the lowest level are not entitled to make decisions regarding recognition of an illegal strike.

In case of a direct threat to life and health of people, the court shall be entitled to suspend a strike that has not started for the period of up to thirty days; in case of a strike in progress, the court can suspend it for the same period.

560. The RF LC states that in cases of vital importance for the interests of the RF or parts of its territory, the Government of the RF is entitled to suspend a strike until the issue of award by the respective court, but not for more than ten calendar days.[232]

561. The award of a court shall be communicated to employees through the head of a striking unit who must immediately inform participants in the strike. Once adopted, the award which acknowledges the strike being unlawful is subject to immediate enforcement. Employees must terminate the strike and return to work not later than the day after the issue of a copy of such award to the head of the striking unit.

562. Participation of an employee in a strike may not be considered as a violation of labour discipline, as well as the ground for dismissal. The exceptions are the cases of non-fulfilment of the liability to terminate a strike which is recognized to be unlawful. Employees must have their employment positions reserved throughout the strike period.

231. The RF Law of 10 Jan. 2003 'On Railway Transport in the Russian Federation' (with subsequent additions and amendments).
232. Article 413 of the RF LC.

563. An employer has the right not to pay wages to employees during the strike period, except for employees engaged in fulfilling the mandatory minimum of accomplishments (services). Any collective agreement reached during the settlement of a collective industrial dispute may provide for compensation due to participating employees.

564. In addition, it is necessary to mention the responsibility of employees for unlawful strikes. Employees who start a strike or fail to terminate it the day after the head of the striking unit was notified of the enacted award acknowledging the strike being unlawful, or adjournment or suspension of the strike, may be subject to disciplinary punishment for infringement of employment discipline.

Regarding the representative unit of the employees which called and failed to terminate the strike thereafter, the liability to indemnify for losses incurred by employer due to the strike at its own expense and in the amount determined by the court exists. In particular a trade union that calls a strike and does not stop it after a court's ruling pronouncing it illegal must compensate from its own funds all the damages caused by the illegal strike.

565. Labour legislation provides the possibility to arrange a specific strike which is called a warning strike. It may be applied as a mean for a collective dispute settlement. A warning strike should be realized in accordance with the following requirements:

(a) It may be called no earlier than five calendar days after the work of the Commission for Conciliation.[233]
(b) It may last only one hour.
(c) It may be announced only once during settlement of a particular collective dispute.
(d) The employer must be given a written notice of three days.
(e) Certainly, during the warning strike the head of the unit must also provide for the minimum of required accomplishments (services) in accordance with the LC.

§3. Statistics

566. Spring 1989 may be recognized as the beginning of industrial action in the USSR. First, some local strikes were organized by miners. Then, they were united into all-country action. Mostly miners protested against changes of their salaries.

Other industries were involved too (e.g., metal workers).

567. Since 1993 strikes have become to be an essential element of the development of labour relations in Russia. Most of them still occur in the coal industry.[234]

---

233. *See* paras 590 and 591.
234. Kazva, A., *Strikes and Other Forms of Collective Protest in Russia in 1997*, <www.alternativy.ru /magazine/htm/98_2/>.

By 1998 the number of strikes had been dramatically increased. In 1993 around 260 enterprises were involved in strikes (the number of participants in strikes was 99,500 employees). In 1998 the same figures were respectively 11,162 and 530,800.[235] In 1998 a high level of industrial actions was registered. Mostly organized by miners, these acquired the status of all-Russian actions of protest.

568. In the beginning of 2000, the activity of employees was reduced. In accordance with Rosstat, in 2003 the number of strikes registered was 67. At the same time, still many employees participated at strikes. As a result of wage arrears, in 2002 more than 3,900 people went on strike in Russia; in the first half of 2003 this figure was equal to 2,300.

569. In 2004 the figures on strikes increased again. For example, in October 2004 the statistic showed 5,907 strikes. That was 80 times more as compared to the entire previous year.[236] Most (96%) strikes were registered in educational sphere (especially, schools). But the number of participants was estimated at 193,500, which means an average 32 participants per strike. The main topic of these strikes was the inadequate level (amount) of salaries.

Recent years reveal a lower level of strikes. For instance, in 2005 at 2,575 enterprises strikes occurred with participation of 84,600 people in total. In 2006 only eight organizations went on strike. And the total number of participants was estimated at 1,200. In 2007 strikes took place in seven organizations, with 2,900 employees involved. In 2011 strikes happened only in two organizations, where in total around 500 employees have participated. The same tendencies are seen during last decade.[237]

235. The Source: Russian Annual Statistic Survey, 1999.
236. *See*<www.virk.ru/news>.
237. Data by the RF Rosstat, *see* //www.gks.ru.

Chapter 6. Settlement of Industrial (Collective) Disputes and Protection of Vital Needs

§1. The Notion of a Collective Dispute

570. The notion of a collective industrial dispute as well as the procedure for settlement of such disputes are regulated by the RF LC.

As was already mentioned before, this Law On Settlement of Collective Disputes was still applicable in accordance with the Article 423 of the LC which until harmonization of laws and other normative legal acts existed in the territory of the RF with the LC. But the rules of the LC have priority.[238]

571. The current LC contains the definition of a collective industrial dispute which reads as an unsettled controversy between employees (their representatives) and employers (their representatives), concerning establishment and change of labour conditions (including remuneration); conclusion, modification and performance of collective agreements, as well as relating to the refusal of an employer to consider the opinion of an elective representative unit of employees for adoption of acts, containing LL norms, within organizations (Article 398 of the LC).

In theory of LL there are also positions which support the idea of classification of collective labour disputes into two groups: conflicts of law and conflicts of interests.[239] For example, disputes regarding establishment of new or hanging of existing conditions of work are viewed as conflicts of interests (which are also called as economical disputes). From the legal point of view, the procedure of settlement of collective labour disputes is applied to such conflicts of interest.

572. Collective disputes may occur at different levels – at an enterprise (its divisions), at levels of industries, etc. It should be stressed that employees of a subsidiary, representative office or other separate structural subdivision of an organization may act as the party to a collective dispute too. The LC also refers to representatives of employees as to the party to a collective dispute.

573. The claims of employees (their representatives) may be raised during negotiating of a collective agreement, as well as in order to change an existing collective agreement; during the process of making of local normative acts (when the legislation requires to take into account the opinion of employees' representatives).

574. The LC describes the procedure of sending of claims by employees (or their representatives). First, the LC enables employees and their representatives to raise claims in framework of a particular collective dispute. Employers, as well their representatives are not competent to raise such claims. Second, such claims must be approved at the respective meeting (or conference) of employees. It is necessary to

238. The RF Law No. 175-FZ of 23 Nov. 1995 'On Procedure of Settlement of Collective Labour Disputes' (with subsequent alterations and additions, mainly in 2001).
239. E.G. Kiselev I.Y., Leonov A.S., *Commentary to the Labour Code of the RF*, – Moscow, 'Delo', 2003. P. 751.

stress that the meeting of employees shall be deemed authorized if the majority of employees are present, whereas the conference shall be deemed authorized provided there being present at least two-thirds of elective delegates.

575. Regarding collective disputes appearing at higher than at an enterprise level, the LC introduced some new rules as compared to the Law on Settlement of Collective Disputes. Trade unions and their associations may raise claims to the respective parties to social partnership. And such claims are not to be approved at the respective meeting (or conference) of employees.

576. Claims of employees shall be made in writing and sent to the employer. The employer is obliged to provide employees or their agents with required premises for the conduct of a meeting (conference) concerning raise of claims, and shall not prevent its conduct. A written copy of claims may be forwarded to the Service for Settlement of Collective Industrial Dispute. In this case the Service is liable to verify to whether the other party to collective industrial dispute has received the claims.

577. The employer engaged in a collective labour dispute must notify the representative body of employees of the organization (subsidiary, representative office or other separate structural subdivision) of his/her decision in writing within three working days of the receipt of such claims. If the claims are forwarded by trade unions (their associations) the agents of employers (associations of employers) are obliged to consider the claims and notify trade unions (their associations) of the adopted decision within a month upon the receipt of such claims. If this procedure is not observed, the collective dispute may arise.

578. In practice, the three following moments are recognized as the beginning of a collective industrial dispute:

(1) the day of issuing of the decision of the employer (his/her representative) to reject the employees' (their representatives) claims, in whole or in part;
(2) the end of the period of sending the decision by the employer regarding the received claims of employees. In particular, Article 400 of the RF LC requires that the employer shall notify a representative unit of employees of organization (subsidiary, representative office or other separate structural subdivision) of his/her decision in writing within three working days of the receipt of such claims; and
(3) the date of making of a dispute report in the course of collective bargaining.

579. The LC states that the procedure of settlement of a collective industrial dispute includes the following steps: consideration of the collective industrial dispute through the Commission for Conciliation, consideration of the dispute through mediation and/or at the Industrial Arbitration (Article 401).

580. The LC requires that the parties' agents, the Commission for Conciliation, the mediator, the Industrial Arbitration and the Service for Settlement of Collective

Industrial Dispute shall use every possibility provided by legislation in order to settle the arisen collective industrial dispute. Strikes are recognized as exceptional means to settle collective disputes.

§2. CONCILIATION

581. Consideration of collective industrial disputes through the Commission for Conciliation is a mandatory step. Only in case of failure to settle the collective industrial dispute through the Commission for Conciliation, the parties shall refer to mediator and/or the labour arbitration. Therefore the three following possibilities of combination of instances in case of settlement of a collective dispute may appear:

(1) the Commission for Conciliation – mediation;
(2) the Commission for Conciliation – labour arbitration; and
(3) the Commission for Conciliation – mediation – labour arbitration.

Meanwhile, each party to a collective industrial dispute may refer at every moment after the beginning of the dispute to the Service for Settlement of Collective Industrial Dispute for notifying registration of the dispute.

582. Conciliation procedures are to be held within established period of time, which may be prolonged upon agreement of the parties to the collective dispute.

583. The Commission for Conciliation should be formed within a period of up to three working days of the beginning of collective industrial dispute. It must include parties' agents on equal rights basis. Parties to collective industrial dispute shall not evade the establishment of the Commission for Conciliation and participation in its work.

584. Collective industrial dispute is administered by the Commission for Conciliation within five working days of the issue of order on its formation. The specified period may be prolonged upon mutual agreement of the parties. It should be confirmed by the form of a protocol. The decision of the Commission for Conciliation shall be adopted upon the parties' agreement, produced in the form of a protocol, and be binding for the parties and subject to enforcement within the terms and times specified by the Commission for Conciliation.

585. For the purposes of making easier the procedure of conciliation the MLSD issued Recommendations on Organization of Work by the Commission for Conciliation (The Decision of the RF MLSD of 14 August 2002).

§3. Mediation

586. If the agreement has not reached at the Commission for Conciliation, the parties shall continue conciliatory procedures with the mediatorand/or by arbitration.

587. According to the RF LC, the parties to a collective industrial dispute may refer to a mediator within three working days. They can choose a mediator by agreement. If necessary, they may refer to the Service for Settlement of Collective Industrial Dispute in order to obtain a recommendation letter concerning candidacy of the mediator.

588. The LC states that the consideration of a collective industrial dispute through the mediator shall be held within a period of up to seven working days from the day of his/her involvement. This step of consideration of the labour dispute may end with the adoption of the agreed decision by the parties to the dispute, or with producing a dispute protocol (Article 403). But mostly the procedures for consideration of a collective industrial dispute through the mediator shall be determined by the parties' agreement with mediator. In this respect the parties involved may use the Recommendations on Organization of Work on a Collective Dispute Settlement with participation of Mediator (the Decision of the MLSD of 14 August 2002).

589. It is necessary to note that if the parties to collective industrial dispute failed to agree upon his/her candidacy within three working days, they shall start formation of labour arbitration. Especially it is important to take into account that the settlement of industrial disputes with participation of mediators is quite rare in the RF.

§4. Arbitration

590. Arbitration is not a mandatory step of settlement of a collective dispute. This rule has exclusions as regard organizations where strikes are banned or restricted by law (*see* paragraphs 557and 558). Formation of labour arbitration is mandatory at such enterprises.

In case of avoidance by either party of participation in the formation or the work of the Commission for Conciliation, the collective industrial dispute shall be referred for consideration to arbitration.

591. The LC (Article 404) refers to some aspects concerning the legal status of labour arbitration. First, it is necessary to stress that labour arbitration is a temporarily existing unit for consideration of a collective industrial dispute: it should be formed in the event that the parties to such dispute have agreed in writing on mandatory enforcement of its decisions. Second, the arbitration shall be arranged by the parties to collective industrial dispute with participation of the Service for Settlement of Collective Industrial Disputes. It is common to involve state servants, in particular, the Service for Settlement of Collective Industrial Disputes to participate in arbitration.

592. Arbitration is to be created not later than three working days after the end of consideration of a collective industrial dispute with the Commission for Conciliation or the mediator. The period of time for acting of arbitration is limited by the LC: the collective industrial dispute shall be considered at the arbitration for up to five working days of its formation.

593. It should be noted that previously arbitration was recognized as an interim body set up by the parties to the dispute and the Service for Settlement of Collective Industrial Disputes. It was composed of three arbitrators recommended by the Service or nominated by the parties to the dispute.

Current legislation does not contain any requirements concerning the number of the participants to arbitration. Formation, membership, standing orders, as well as competence of the arbitration shall be formally validated by a joint decision of the employer, the employees' representatives and the specified Service. There are also Recommendations on Organization of Work on a Collective Dispute Settlement at Labour Arbitration (the Decision of the MLSD of 14 August 2002) which may be used by the parties involved to create the Regulations on arbitration.

594. Written recommendations of the arbitration concerning settlement of collective industrial dispute should be provided to the parties involved.

595. LL provides the guarantees for persons engaged in the settlement of collective industrial dispute (Article 405 of the LC). The guaranties include reservation of working place and limitations of an employer in the sphere of applying of disciplinary sanction. In particular the members of the Commission for Conciliation and industrial arbitrators, while considering collective industrial dispute, shall be relieved from their principal employment with their average wage being reserved, for a period of not more than three months in one year. Representatives of employees, their associations participating in a settlement of collective industrial dispute, shall not be, for the period of the settlement, the subject to any disciplinary punishment, as well as they may not be re-engaged or dismissed without prior consent of the authorizing body. It should be stressed that the above guarantees are not given to mediators.

§5. The Role of the Government

I. State Service for Collective Dispute Settlements

596. For the purposes of resolving of collective labour disputes the Service for Collective Disputes Settlement (as included into the MLSP) was established. Its statutes were approved by the Decision of the RF Government of 15 April 1996.[240]

597. The current LC states that public services for settlement of collective industrial disputes are realized by federal state authorities, which are formed as part of the federal executive body of labour (now – the RF MLSP), as well as by the respective executive bodies of the subjects of the RF. They assist in settlement of collective industrial dispute through conciliatory procedures and participation in them.

The LC (Article 407) describes the following competence of the federal bodies mentioned above. In particular the federal state body of executive power, realizing the functions in the sphere of collective labour disputes resolving, is entitled in the following fields of activity:

(1) to provide notifying registration of collective industrial disputes;
(2) to produce a list of industrial arbitrators;
(3) to carry on training of industrial arbitrators majoring in settlement of collective industrial disputes;
(4) to grant systematic assistance to the parties to collective industrial disputes throughout the whole process of settlement of such dispute; and
(5) to assist in the sphere of settlement of industrial disputes.

598. The employees of the above-mentioned public bodies have the right, upon presentation of appropriate certificate, of unimpeded visit of a work area pertaining to the dispute (subsidiary, representative office or any other separate structural subdivision) for the purpose of settlement of a collective industrial dispute, finding and elimination of reasons giving birth to such disputes.

II. Labour Arbitration Court

599. Some special institutions have been established for the purposes of arbitration in subjects of the RF. In particular in the framework of the social partnership system in Moscow for the first time in the RF, a specialized structure for settlement of collective labour disputes – the Labour Arbitration Court – was founded. It was established by the Resolution of the Moscow Government dated of 11 September 2001[241] in the framework of the international TACIS project.

The founders of this labour arbitration are the following institutions:

240. The Decision of the Government of the RF of 1996, as amended in 1998.
241. The Resolution No. 840-PP 'On Establishment of the Institution Labour Arbitration Court for Collective Labour Dispute Settlement'.

(a) the Committee for Public Relations of Moscow (as a representative of the Government of Moscow);
(b) the Moscow Federation of Trade Unions;
(c) the Moscow Confederation of Industrialists and Businessmen (Employers); and
(d) lawyers.

600. The Labour Arbitration Court consists of fifty persons, representing employers, trade unions, executive authorities, scientists and practicing lawyers.

The main fields of activity of the Labour Arbitration Court are the following:

(1) consultative and practical support in settlement of collective labour disputes with participation in the labour arbitration;
(2) increasing of the level of professional knowledge of experts in the field of settlement of collective labour disputes; and
(3) participating in development and analysis of draft laws, belonging to labour legislation, and in revision of the current legal acts in view of experience and recommendations of the ILO, provisions of conventions of the ILO, generally accepted international practice and obligations of the RF in the framework of international agreements and so on.

III. Courts and State Labour Inspection

601. It has to be mentioned that the RF LC does not prescribe participation of courts in settlement of collective labour disputes. But in some particular cases, it is allowed to involve courts and administrative state bodies into the appropriate procedures. For example, Article 357, Part 2 of the LC provides a possibility of an appeal to the Labour Inspection by a trade union, an employee, or other person, on the issue, processed by the respective body, examining collective labour disputes. The State Labour Inspector, upon the disclosure of an infringement of the LC or other legal acts, containing labour regulations, has the right to charge an employer with a binding directive. The employer has the right to appeal to the court. But obviously, it will be another procedure, which is not equal to the settlement of a collective industrial dispute and which does not exclude the last one.

Selected Bibliography

Legislation

Russian federal legislation is published in official journals *Sobraniye Zakonodatel'stva*, *Parlamentskaya Gazeta* and *Rossiyskaya Gazeta.*

Federal legislation, as well as legislation of the subjects of the RF may be also found in legal databases inInternet. The most famous database of Russian legislation (in Russian, as well as in English) is 'Garant'. *See*<www.garant.ru>.

The text of the RF Constitution is available at www.constitution.ru/en

Court Practice

A selection of the RF Supreme Court is published in *Bulletin Verkhovnogo Suda RF*. The appropriate decisions also may be referred to legal databases on the Internet <www.supcourt.ru/vs_docs.php>.

Constitutional Court Surveys are published in *Vestnik Konstitutsionnogo Suda RF. See also*<http://ks.rfnet.ru/>.

Current Statistics and Other Information

Some statistical and analytic reports are taken from periodicals such as *Economika i Jizn*; *Rossiyskaya Gazeta.*

The official source of statistics are issued by Rosstat of the RF (previously – Goskomstat). This state body issues statistical collections and reports on the social and economic situation of the RF (monthly, quarterly in the case of small enterprises and annual). In particular, the following issues contain the information on statistic *Socioeconomic position in Russia* (monthly, Moscow); *Socioeconomic position in Russia* (monthly, Moscow); and *Current Statistical Survey* (quarterly). *Handbook Russia* (annual). Some statistical information is available inInternet. *See* <www.gks.ru>.

Both statistic and analytical reports are found in the following sources:

- publications of World Bank <www.worldbank.org/html/dec/Publications/Workpapers>;
- regarding data about economy *see* <www.economy.gov.ru>;
- Russian European Centre for Economic Policy (RECEP): Russian Economic Trends (quarterly, with monthly updates; Moscow). Website: <www.hhs.se/site/ret/ret.htm>.

Information on the status and structure of the state bodies if the RF is provided by the following sources:

<www.gov.ru/main/page8.html>;
<www.council.gov.ru/index_e.htm> (the Council of Federation of the Federal Assembly of the Russian Federation);
<www.gov.ru/> (the RF Government);
<http://president.kremlin.ru> (the President of the RF);
<www.supcourt.ru/EN/index.htm> (the Supreme Court of the Russian Federation).
www.rosmintrud.ru

Regarding Trade Union status and activity *see*:

<www.trud.org/> – in Russian;
<www.trud.org/index7.htm> – in English;
www.vkt.org.ru/history_eng.htm; and
www.fmpr.ru.

For the data on the status of employers' representatives, *see* <www.rspp.biz/eng>.

Books in Russian

Alexandrov, N.G., *Trudovoye pravootnosheniye/Employment Relationship/*, Moscow, 1948.
Commentary to the RFLC: Red Orlosvsky, J.P. Moscow: 'Intra-M-Kontrakt', 2009.
Getman-Pavlova, I. *Mezhdunarodnoye Chastnoye Pravo/*International Private Law, Moscow, Jurait, 2013.
Gorbacheva, Zh. A., *Vvodniy kommentariy k trudovomu kodeksu/Brief Commentary to the Labour Code/*, Moscow: 'MCFR', 2002.
Kiselev, I.Y., *Mejdunarofniy trud/International Labour*, Moscow, 1997. Moscow: MGU, 1989.
Kiselev, I.Y., *Sravnitelnoye i mejdunarodnoye trudovoye pravo/*Comparative and International Labour Law/, Moscow, 1999.
Kiselev, I.Y., Leonov, A.S., *Kommentariy k trudovomu kodeksu Rossii/Commentary to the Labour Code of the RF*, Moscow: 'Delo', 2003.
Kurennoy, A.M., *Trudovoe pravo na puti k rynku/Labour Law on the Way to Market*, Moscow: 'Delo', 1997.

Kurennoy, A.M., *Trudovyie spori: prakticheskiy kommentariy./Labour Disputes: Practical Commentary*, Moscow: 'Delo', 2001.

Mavrin, S.P., Khohlov, E.B., and others, *Kurs Rossiyskogo trudovogo prava/The Course of Russian Labour Law/*, in 2 parts, Moscow, 2001.

Lushnikov, A.M., *Nauka trudovogo prava: istoriko-pravovoy ocherk v litsah i sobytiyah/The Science of Labour Law in Russia: Historical-legal Outline in Faces and Events*, Moscow, 2003.

Lushnikov, A.M., Lushnikova, M.V., *Kurs trudovogo prava/The Course on Labour Law/*, Textbook, Part 1, Moscow: 'Prospect', 2003; Part 2, Moscow 'Prospect', 2004.

Mavrin, S.P., *Sovremennyie problemy obchei chasti rossiyskogo trudovogo prava/ Contemporary Problems of General Part of Russian Labour Law*, S-Petersburg, 1993.

Orlovskiy, J.P. (ed.) and others. *Kommentariy k trudovomy kodeksu RF/Commentary to the RF LC*, Moscow: 'Infra-M-Kontrakt', 2009.

Skobelkin, V.N., *Trudovyie pravootnosheniya/Employment Relationships,/* Moscow, 1999.

Snigireva, I.O., *Profsoyuzy i trudovoye pravo/Trade-unions and Labour Law/*, Moscow, 1983.

Tal, L.S., *Trudovoi dogovor: tsivilisticheskoye issledovanie/Employment Contract: Civil Law Research/*, Yaroslavl, 1913.

Trudovoe pravo i pravo socialnogo obespecheniya: Aktualnie problemi/Labour Law and Social Security: Modern Problems/Moskovskaia Gosudarstvennaia Juridicheskaia Akademia. Moskva, 2000.

Mavrin, S, Savonov, V., *Trudovoj Kodex* /Labour Code of the RF with Comments, Moscow, 2017.

Trudovoye pravo Rossii/Labour Law of Russia (*Textbook*), Moscow: Moscow State University, 'Jurist', 2008.

Books in English, German

Braguinsky, S., Yavlinsky, G., *Incentives and Institutions: The Transition to a Market Economy in Russia*. Princeton, N.J.: Princeton University Press, 2000.

Brödermann, Rosengarten. Internationales Privat- und Zivilverfahrensrecht. Vahlen München, 2015.

Christensen, Paul T., *Russia's Workers in Transition: Labour, Management, and the State Under Gorbachev and Yeltsin*, Dekalb: Northern Illinois University Press, 1999.

Clarke, S., *The Formation of a Labour Market in Russia*, Cheltenham, UK; Northampton, MA: Edward Elgar, 1999.

Cook, L.J., *Labour and Liberalization: Trade Unions in the New Russia*. New York: Twentieth Century Fund Press, 1997.

Gender Issues at Work: Case Studies on Russian Enterprises, ILO Geneva, 2000.

Hoffer, F., *Traditional Trade Unions During Transition and Economic Reform in the Russian Federation*. Interdepartmental Action Programme on Privatization,

Restructuring and Economic Democracy; Enterprise and Cooperative Development Dept., International Labour Office. Geneva, ILO, 1997. Osakwe, Ch., Russian *Civil Code, Annotated Translation and Commentary* by, Moscow: 'Moscow State University Press Publishers', 2000.

Thirkell, J.E.M., Petkov, K., and Vickerstaff, S.A., *The Transformation of Labour Relations: Restructuring and Privatization in Eastern Europe and Russia.* Oxford, New York: Oxford University Press, 1998.

Articles and Contributions to Books in Russian

Bugrov, L.U., T Ponyatie i classifikatsiya soglasheniy po rossiyskomu trudovomu pravu/The notion and classification of agreements under Russian Labour Law/, *State and Law*, 2002, No. 4.

Gorbacheva, Zh. A., Labour market and legal regulation of promotion of employment, in: *Labour Law of Russia (Textbook), Moscow: Moscow State University*, 'Jurist', 2004.

Gorbacheva, Zh. A., Legal regulation of employment in Russia in the light of drafting Labour Code. – *Digest of International Labour Organization, Moscow Office*, 2001.

Kazva, A., *Strikes and OtherForms of CollectiveProtest in Russia in 1997.* <www.alternativy.ru/magazine/htm/98_2/strikes.htm>.

Orlovskiy, Y.P., The Labour Code of the RF. //'*Khozyaistvo i Pravo*', 2002, No. 3.

Articles in English

Blasi, J., Panina, D., Emerging industrial relations system in Russia's privatized enterprises. *Labour Law Journal* (Chicago) 45 (8), August 1994.

Bliss, Amy J., Proletariat to perestroika: a comparison of Labour Law in the Soviet Union and the Russian Federation. *Comparative Labour Law Journal*, Volume 18, Number 2, Winter 97.

Egorov, V., Privatization and labour relations in the countries of Central and Eastern Europe. *Industrial Relations Journal*. Volume 27, No. 1, March 1996

Egorov, V.V., The reform of Soviet labour legislation: problems and prospects. *Columbia Journal of Transitional Law*, Vol. 28, No. 1, 1990.

Gorbacheva, Zh. A., The autonomy of collective agreements, *Bulletin of Comparative Labour Relations*, 2003, No. 48.

Index

The numbers here refer to paragraph numbers

Made in the USA
Monee, IL
18 October 2026

66041384R10116